OUR STAFF

Building Our Human Resources

Trish Holford

Augsburg Fortress
Minneapolis

OUR STAFF
Building Our Human Resources

Developed in cooperation with the Division for Congregational Ministries of the Evangelical Lutheran Church in America, Michael R. Rothaar, project manager.

Scripture quotations are from New Revised Standard Version Bible, copyright © 1989 Division of Christian Education of the National Council of the Churches of Christ in the United States of America. Used by permission.

Portions of chapters 2 and 3 are adapted from *Managing Risks, First Steps in Identifying Congregational Liability*, Richard B. Couser, copyright © 1993 Augsburg Fortress.

Series overview: David P. Mayer, Michael R. Rothaar
Editors: Laurie J. Hanson, James Satter

Cover design and series logo: Marti Naughton
Text design: James Satter
Cover photograph: Gordon Gray, FRPS

About the cover image: The centerpiece of the Resurrection Window in First Lisburn Presbyterian Church, Northern Ireland, was created by stained glass artist James Watson, Belfast, from fragments of church windows destroyed by a car bomb in 1981 and restored after a second bomb in 1989. The window symbolizes new life in Christ, which transforms darkness to light, hatred to love, despair to hope, and death to life. The members of First Lisburn Presbyterian have lived out this promise through new initiatives for community service, reconciliation, and peace-making.

ISBN 0-8066-4410-9

The paper used in this publication meets the minimum requirements of American National Standard for Information Sciences—Permanence of Paper for Printed Library Materials, ANSI Z329.48-1984.

Manufactured in the U.S.A.

06   05   04   03   02   1   2   3   4   5   6   7   8   9   10

✛ Contents

Series Overview

Welcome to the Congregational Leader Series, and welcome to the journey of discovering God's future for you and your congregation. Your congregation's mission and ministry are given to you by God. We sometimes refer to "our church," but it is always Christ's church. We are at best its stewards or caretakers, not its owners. As we plan, organize, and lead, we strive toward excellence in everything we do to reflect the glory and grace of God, who has entered human life to redeem us.

As a congregational leader, you may be asking, "What is our mission? How should we structure things? How can we plan for the future and where will the resources come from?" The Congregational Leader Series provides resources for effective planning and leadership development. Each book includes biblical and theological foundations for planning and leadership development, and practical information to use in building on your congregation's strengths.

We are first of all called to be faithful to God's word and will. Exploring the Bible enables us to discern what God's plan is for us as individuals and as a congregation. Ignoring or minimizing the centrality of God in our deliberations risks not only failure but also our faith. In the words of the psalmist, "Unless the LORD builds the house, those who build it labor in vain" (Psalm 127:1).

Why should we engage in congregational planning and leadership development? When the congregation is at its best, these activities aid us in fulfilling our mission to the world: reaching out with the gospel of Jesus Christ. Faithful planning for mission mirrors God's activity in the world, from creating and covenant-making to gathering and renewing the church. When congregations fail to plan, they risk dissipating the resources they have been given by God and begin falling away from all that God has intended for them.

In short, faithful planning and leadership development engage the congregation and all its members in the creative work of God. Continually analyzing and shaping our vision, mission, ministry, and context allows us to ask, "What is God calling our congregation to be?" Working to develop and support leaders enables us to ask, "How has God gifted each of us for ministry?"

We begin with prayer

As congregational leaders, we always begin our endeavors with prayer. Discerning God's will for us is a task that requires that we be in communication with God. Unfortunately, we often come up with new ideas and programs—and then pray that God will bless them! That order needs to be reversed. Our prayers should precede our plans, helping us discern God's call to us.

As congregational leaders, we always begin our endeavors with prayer.

In his few years of public ministry, Jesus accomplished a tremendous amount of healing, teaching, and service for others. However, his ministry did not begin until after he had spent an extended period of time in the wilderness reflecting on his call and God's purpose for his life. Following that retreat, virtually every moment of his life's story was punctuated with prayer and ultimately concluded with his supplications in Gethsemane and on the cross.

Paul wrote to the Thessalonians, "Rejoice always, pray without ceasing, give thanks in all circumstances; for this is the will of God in Christ Jesus for you" (1 Thessalonians 5:16-18). These words were meant for us—congregational leaders anxious to get on with things that need to be done. Notice how Paul places *prayer* between *rejoice* and *thanks* in this verse. Prayer is not simply another task to be done nor an obligation to be met. It is a gift of God to be celebrated and used with joy and thanksgiving. It is meant to permeate our lives. As leaders, we are seeking to construct God's will in our communities. God invites us to build with gladness and to make prayer the mortar between every brick we lay.

We build from strength

Most leadership resources begin with the assumption that there is a problem to be solved. In the midst of the real problems that surround us, however, our task as congregational leaders is to identify the strengths, giftedness, and blessings that God has given to us and the congregation. Our primary calling is not to be problem-solvers but to be asset-builders. Paul reminds us, "Let all things be done for building up"(1 Corinthians 14:26). This is not license to ignore problems, conflicts, or deficiencies. Rather, it is a call to view the brokenness around us in a new way.

Our role as Christian leaders is to attempt to look at our congregation, our fellow Christians, and ourselves, as God sees us. "This is my commandment, that you love one another as I have loved you" (John 15:12). Jesus did not blindly ignore the problems around him. Instead, he viewed those problems through a lens of love, appreciation, and forgiveness. We are called to build from strength, to construct our plans and visions from what God has given us. When we try to build from weakness and focus only on our problems, we compound both and ultimately fail.

> **Our primary calling is not to be problem-solvers but to be asset-builders.**

First Church was located in a growing, well-to-do suburb, on a main thoroughfare, and in a beautiful new building. The members of First Church appeared to have everything going for them, and the congregation's future looked very bright.

The congregation, however, faced an ongoing problem with mortgage payments. This problem became so all-consuming that the congregation began to lose sight of its strengths, gifts, and mission for the future. The members of First Church had everything they needed to solve the problem of mortgage payments but they were unable to stop fixating on it. Soon, many other issues surfaced as everyone became a fault-finder.

Today there is no mortgage-payment problem because there is no First Church. The preoccupation with weakness and deficiency blinded the congregation to the reality of its gifts. This congregation died, not because of its problems but because of its perspective.

We must constantly ask ourselves and others, "Where is God at work here? What gifts have we received for ministry in this place?" Focusing only on what we don't have breeds jealousy, competition, hopelessness, and lost vision. Focusing on our gifts gives birth to joy, affirmation, and hope.

We won't find quick fixes

We live in a culture obsessed with quick fixes and mesmerized by the notion that there is a prescription for every ailment and accident. But things keep falling apart. People get sick. Programs fail. Committees don't function. Plans backfire. And goals aren't met. The list of mistakes, failures, misfires, and flops grows and grows. In his letter to the Romans, Paul reminds us that "all have sinned and fall short of the glory of God" (Romans 3:23). Paul says this not to weigh us down with despair, but instead to remind us that our salvation comes from God and not ourselves.

Faithful leaders have a deep respect for the reality of problems and obstacles. Things will always fall apart. That's why planning, assessing, goal-setting, leading, and visioning are ongoing processes, not quick fixes. As leaders, we need to know the nature of sin and publicly acknowledge its pervasiveness. Then we can lead, not with unhealthy fatalism, but with honesty, humility, and a sense of humor.

We are all ministers

As Christians, everything we do and plan is communal. We cannot plan unilaterally or devise strategies in isolation. To be sure, each of us has received salvation individually through baptism, but at that moment, through the water and the Word, we were united with the body of Christ. Even the gifts that God has given each of us are meant for the common good of all God's people: "To each is given the manifestation of the Spirit for the common good" (1 Corinthians 12:7).

In other words, each of us is a minister, whether pastor or lay person, and each of us is called to serve others. This is a radical departure from our culture's overwhelming emphasis on individual

Each of us is a minister, whether pastor or lay person, and each of us is called to serve others.

independence. The idea that we are all ministers and that as the church we minister as a community has tremendous implications for all of our planning and development efforts.

Leadership development is nothing more than equipping the members of the congregation so that they are strengthened for ministry: "The gifts he gave were that some would be apostles, some prophets, some evangelists, some pastors and teachers, to equip the saints for the work of ministry, for building up the body of Christ" (Ephesians 4:11-12). Paul would be appalled at the idea that a paid professional minister should carry out all of the ministry of the congregation or that only some people in the congregation are called to ministry.

Faithful planning and leadership development affirm that all of God's people are gifted and invited to participate in ministry. Identifying, embracing, and strengthening each other's gifts for common mission is a daunting task that never ends, but through that effort and in that journey we become what God intended: "But you are a chosen race, a royal priesthood, a holy nation, God's own people, in order that you may proclaim the mighty acts of him who called you out of darkness into his marvelous light" (1 Peter 2:9).

A model for understanding congregations

Congregations are extremely complex. Throughout the Congregational Leader Series, we invite you to look at your congregation through a particular model or set of lenses. This model helps us to understand why congregations are so complex, and it provides some important clues for the leadership skills and tasks that are needed.

A congregation resembles three different institutions at the same time: a *community of spiritual formation*, a *voluntary association*, and a *nonprofit organization*. This isn't a matter of size—the largest and smallest are alike in this. It isn't a matter of context—the model applies to both urban and rural settings. Each type of institution has different values and goals, which may even contradict each other. Each of these values and goals requires different things from leaders.

Communities of spiritual formation

A congregation is, in part, a community of spiritual formation. People come to such a community to join with others in growing closer to God. They seek to understand God's word and God's will for their life. They seek an experience of God's presence, a spiritual or emotional awareness of transcendence and love. They seek time for contemplation and prayer, and also time to work with others on tasks that extend God's love to others.

How are our congregations communities of spiritual formation? Much of congregational life centers on worship. We teach children and adults the practice of faith. The church provides support in Christ's name during times of crisis and need. We engage in visible and public activities, such as offering assistance to people who are homeless, or hungry, or survivors of abuse, as a way of both serving God and proclaiming God's mercy and justice.

The most important value in a community of spiritual formation is authenticity.

The most important value in a community of spiritual formation is authenticity. There is no room for pretense, no room for manipulation, and no room for power games. The goals we establish must be clearly directed to outcomes in people's spiritual lives. The fundamental question for self-evaluation is this: "How has our ministry brought people closer to God?"

Voluntary associations

Like any club or voluntary association, a congregation is a gathering of people who are similar to one another in specific ways, share a common purpose, and largely govern and finance their organization's existence and activities. In addition, people often find that belonging to a club is a way to make friends and social or business contacts, and enjoy meaningful leisure time activities. Some voluntary associations, such as Kiwanis or Lions clubs, have charitable purposes and sometimes seek support from people beyond their own membership. Some voluntary associations are focused on common interests or activities, such as gardening or providing youth athletic leagues.

Membership requirements may be strict or fluid, costs may be high or low, and commitments may be long or short, but they are spelled out rather clearly. A number of unwritten rules may serve to get people to conform to common values. Most voluntary associations would like to have more members, both to strengthen their organization and to expand the social benefits that come from a broader circle. But the new members usually are people who are very much like those who are already members.

The most important value in a voluntary association is effectiveness in helping people relate to one another.

The most important value in a voluntary association is effectiveness in helping people relate to one another. The goals are largely relational. There must be many opportunities for people to form relationships, especially with those with whom they have much in common. The association must operate in such a way that people all feel that their own values and hopes are being well served, usually through direct access to the decision-making process and ample opportunities for public dissent. People want and expect to be contacted regularly by both leaders and other members, and to feel that they are fully accepted as part of the group.

It is also important that there is a consensus—a shared vision—on what the association is and does. When conflict emerges, it must be negotiated and resolved. Because membership is voluntary, when there's conflict, or when they just don't feel part of the group anymore, people are usually quick to withhold their financial support or quit altogether.

Nonprofit organizations

As if it weren't complicated enough to be both a community of spiritual formation and a voluntary association, now consider that your congregation is also a nonprofit organization. It is a chartered or incorporated institution, recognized as a legal entity by the federal, state, and municipal government. A congregation can borrow and lend, sue and be sued. You as a congregation are accountable to society and responsible for following all applicable laws. Almost all congregations are property owners and employers. The congregation has formal operational procedures and documents (from your constitution to state laws) that dictate how you must make decisions and conduct your affairs. The usually unspoken but fundamental goal of a nonprofit organization is self-perpetuation, making sure that the institution will continue.

In this regard, congregations are similar to any business that offers services to the public. Being *nonprofit* simply means that the organization's assets can't be distributed to individuals or for purposes contrary to the charter. It doesn't mean that the congregation can't or shouldn't be run in a businesslike manner—or that it can't accumulate assets. The actual operation doesn't differ much from that of a profit-making business. In a nonprofit organization, the primary value is efficiency, or achieving the greatest results with the least possible expenditure of resources.

Another core value is continuity, with orderly systems that must be applied by anyone who carries out the organization's work. To reach financial goals, a nonprofit organization seeks voluntary contributions and often regularizes revenue through endowments and ancillary sources of income. Efforts are made to minimize costs without sacrificing quality. The organization also tries to build reserves to meet unanticipated circumstances and periodic needs (such as replacement of depreciating assets). Policies are in place to protect the staff and volunteers, and to ensure clear and mutually agreed upon expectations. There are clear lines of accountability and each person operates within a specified scope of decision-making.

Planning in a nonprofit organization includes making the best use of property and facilities. The property is seldom an end in itself, but the goal of leadership is always to maximize its usefulness. Other organizational goals revolve around having a truly public presence, including marketing effectively, identifying the needs and wants of a particular group of people, developing a product or service that addresses those needs, and informing the target group of its desirability and availability. Nonprofit organizations must do this as surely and skillfully as those in the profit sector.

In a nonprofit organization, the primary value is efficiency, or achieving the greatest results with the least possible expenditure of resources.

You may have heard that "you shouldn't be a manager, you should be a leader." This is unfortunate language, because management is part of leadership, and voluntary organizations need managers. How you analyze, organize, delegate, supervise, and evaluate the congregation's work is critical to its vitality.

Leadership

What does the word *leadership* really mean? Think of it as having three dimensions: *character*, *knowledge*, and *action*. *Character* permeates all three aspects of this model. Leaders have principles and try to live them out. In any of the three ways in which we're looking at congregations, leaders are honest, trustworthy, dedicated, caring, disciplined, and faithful to the core principles—and have many more virtues as well. Although everyone sins and fails, be clear that improvement is expected from all leaders.

It is not only character that counts. Leaders must also know things and do things. *Knowledge* and *action* can be developed. They can be learned in books and classes or from working with people who have expertise. Things we know from one part of our experience can be applied to other parts of our lives.

Applying the congregational model

The three-part model of congregations is helpful in exploring the different things that leaders must be, know, and do in a community of spiritual formation, in a voluntary association, and in a nonprofit organization.

Problems develop when the values, goals, and leadership styles appropriate to one part of the congregational model are mistakenly applied to one of the others. It is not wrong to value authentic spirituality, effective interpersonal relationships, and operational efficiency. There are times when each of these should be given the highest priority. Recognize that your congregation probably has emphasized one of these areas at the expense of the others, and plan your way to a better balance. Embrace the wonderful complexity of congregational life and ask God to move among us to change us and renew us and rededicate us to God's own purposes.

The Congregational Leader Series

This is one of several books in the Congregational Leader Series. The entire series seeks to build on the positive, basing your planning on assets rather than deficiencies, and to focus on outcomes, enabling your congregation to make a specific and definable difference in people's lives. The series has two sets: congregational planning and leadership development. Books in this series can be used in any order, so you can get started with those books that are most helpful for you and your congregation. The reproducible tools can be used with your council, committees, planning teams, leadership groups, and other members of the congregation. Visit www.augsburgfortress.org/CLS to download and customize these tools.

Faithful planning and leadership development take us on a journey, a pilgrimage, and an exploration of God's possibilities for you and your congregation. The Congregational Leader Series provides resources for your travels, as you seek God's will and guidance for you and your congregation.

This image of a cross indicates that further information on a topic appears in another book in the Congregational Leader Series.

Acknowledgments

The making of this book models its message. It took many voices with many different gifts. Without each of these voices of wisdom, help, and encouragement, this book would not exist.

My thanks to the individuals who generously participated in a survey or provided insight into a particular ministry area. They represent varied temperaments, ministries, positions, congregation sizes, and locations. They are laity and clergy serving on the churchwide staff of the Evangelical Lutheran Church in America, synod staffs, program staffs, administrative staffs, technical staffs, or facilities staffs: Lisa Arrington, Dick Bruesehoff, Diane Crider, Anne Durboraw, Nancy Easton, David Helfrich, Jim Helm, Susan Hively, Suzanne House, Brian Hughes, Lee Hulsether, Richard Krebs, Susan Lang, Monte Leister, Dennis Nelson, Tim Robertson, Ray Scheck, and Robert Wallace.

There are numerous other people who shared their stories and soul-felt discernments with me through the years. I am grateful for their examples of openness and determination to serve their congregations. In congregations everywhere, there are staff members going to work, seeking daily to do the work of the gospel. This book recognizes the hard and dedicated work of all staff members. In particular, I extend hearty thanks to my current coworkers for their help and support during the writing process, with special gratitude to the head of our staff, Dave Helfrich. His passion for the gospel message, dedication to a ministry of growth and innovation, and constant support of this writing project reflect essential pieces needed for healthy and vibrant staff team ministry.

Finally, my thanks to my husband, Jim, for his incredible love, enduring patience, and encouragement, not only as this book was written but during all the years that I have served as a congregational staff member. Truly, I haven't served alone!

Introduction

One day the disciples were walking with Jesus on the road to Jerusalem. Jesus was telling them what was going to happen to him in that city. James and John came forward and asked Jesus to fulfill a request for them. "Be specific," he answered.

"Can we be your two top guys and share in your glory?"

Jesus may have sighed as he said, "You don't understand." He went on to explain to them, and the other 10 followers who came up and clamored to be part of the conversation, that the road before their teacher was one they could only follow if they understood that they were called "not to be served but to serve" (Mark 10:45).

We are all called to serve. This book looks at the standard set forth by Jesus as it relates to staff and staffing issues that affect local congregations. What does it mean to have a staff in a congregation? Are staff members different from other members and leaders in the congregation? Why should we pay some people for what others are doing as volunteers?

This book is part of the Congregational Leader Series, which examines critical areas in strategic planning and leadership development. The topics of the books in the series are interdependent and often overlap in the day-to-day life of a congregation. For instance, to staff correctly, you need to understand the mission of the organization, how financial assets are considered and allocated, and boundaries of authority and responsibility. These understandings are crucial whether you are looking at staffing a new entrepreneurial undertaking, a large established corporation, or a non-profit enterprise such as the local congregation.

The early church

In Acts 6, the early church experiences rapid growth. As a result, it struggles with who will do what:

During this time, as the disciples were increasing in numbers by leaps and bounds, hard feelings developed among the Greek-speaking believers—"Hellenists"—toward the Hebrew speaking believers because their widows were being discriminated against in the daily food lines. So the Twelve called a meeting of the disciples. They said, "It wouldn't be right for us to abandon our responsibilities for preaching and teaching the Word of God to help with the care of the poor. So, friends, choose seven men from among you whom everyone trusts, men full of the Holy Spirit and good sense, and we'll assign them this task. Meanwhile, we'll stick to our assigned task of prayer and speaking God's word.

The congregation thought this was a great idea. They went ahead and chose—Stephen, a man full of faith and the Holy Spirit, Philip, Procorus, Nicanor, Timon, Parmenas, Nicolas, a convert from Antioch.

Then they presented them to the apostles. Praying, the apostles laid on hands and commissioned them for their task.

The Word of God prospered. The number of disciples in Jerusalem increased dramatically. Not least, a great many priests submitted themselves to the faith.

—Acts 6:1-7, in Eugene H. Peterson,
The Message, The New Testament in Contemporary English,
Colorado Springs: NavPress, 1993, p. 249

The early church was challenged to see that all the needs of all the people were addressed. The twelve disciples called a meeting of the community and discussed the need and the solution. Their answer was that more people were needed to do specific duties that would be part of how they identified and accomplished ministry in that particular time and place.

Early Protestant churches in the United States

Early Protestant churches in the United States faced the same challenge of accomplishing tasks that were essential to their ministry. Generally, pastors were seen as the only ones who needed to be compensated for the work that they performed on behalf of congregations. This compensation came in the form of foodstuffs, other material items, or parsonages owned by the local congregation or larger church.

An increase in paid staff positions

In the last decades, there has been an increase in paid staff positions in local congregations in almost all mainline denominations. Congregations have added paid staff members in a variety of positions: Christian education directors, administrative assistants, custodians, youth directors, organists, choir directors, music ministers, contemporary worship leaders, parish nurses, pastoral counselors, volunteer coordinators, small group care facilitators,

For the purposes of this book, the term *staff* is used here to describe laity who have been employed by a local congregation and receive financial and/or other material compensation for the work they do on behalf of the congregation's ministries.

Being employed and compensated means that staff members have a unique relationship with the members of the congregation who work alongside them in the congregation's ministries and are in a position to contribute to staff compensation.

Clergy and lay staff members working together in a congregation will be referred to as a *staff team*.

family ministry coordinators, business administrators, facilities managers, financial planners, and information or worship technology specialists.

One reason for this increase in paid staff positions is that the local pastor cannot provide all of the ministry leadership needed in a congregation singlehandedly. Pastors may not have the time available to accomplish everything that needs to be done. Added to this, they may not have all of the skills necessary to fulfill those needs.

The changing nature of the volunteer base of the local congregation has also meant an increase in paid staff positions. Jobs and daily commutes, children, health issues, sports and recreation, and other commitments may place demands on the time of church members. The number of available volunteer hours that individuals are able or willing to give to their congregations is shrinking.

In direct conflict with the volunteerism of their parents in the "builder" generation, some "baby boomers" are more willing to give dollars than their time to the needs of a congregation. People in the builder generation, and the generations before it, were at the church on Saturday mornings to clean the building, wash the windows, repair the furnace, and paint what was peeling. Baby boomers are more inclined to hire a cleaning service or a custodian to clean and a vendor to paint.

Time is the currency of the future.

In *Soul Tsunami* (Grand Rapids: Zondervan, 1999, p. 272), author Leonard Sweet has suggested that if money was the currency of the past, then time is the currency of the future that is emerging today. Nowhere does the church feel this more than in the diminishing time that even very dedicated and well-intentioned members are willing to give to their congregation.

As the church has faced this challenge, one solution has been to use paid staff to fill responsibilities that in decades past may have been carried out solely by volunteers. These staff members have their work time allotted to complete the tasks that need to be accomplished.

Staff members and volunteers

No congregation can survive without the many committed volunteers who not only serve in ministry, but are also in fact the visible body of Christ, simply by their presence. Volunteers, the members in the pews, are the congregation, reaching out in the name of the local congregation and in the name of Jesus Christ.

Ephesians 4:15-16 reminds us that "speaking the truth in love, we must grow up in every way into him who is the head, into Christ, from whom the whole body, joined and knit together by every ligament with which it is equipped, as each part is working properly, promotes the body's growth in building itself up in love." Staff members and volunteers *together* comprise the priesthood of all believers for the local congregation. Both are essential for the local congregation. When staff members and volunteers take seriously their ministry together, their joint efforts can build up the local body of Christ and further the cause of sharing the gospel with all.

Staff members and volunteers *together* comprise the priesthood of all believers for the local congregation.

Dependability, accountability, and frustrations

"Well, I just can't make it in today to help. My aunt just phoned to say she is dropping by and she needs me to help her with her medications. I'm sorry. Maybe I can help next week."

"I would really love to be at the next meeting of the youth ministry, but right now I am taking an evening computer class."

"I wish I could sing with the choir this year, but my job schedule has me traveling more than ever and I know I would miss more rehearsals than I would make."

Words similar to these have been heard in every congregation, sometimes from members who are very dedicated to their congregation's ministry. Volunteers can say "yes" or "no" to ministry opportunities at their own discretion. It is very important that we honor their right to make their own decisions.

Another factor in dealing with volunteerism is burnout. What has been called the 20-80 rule, or the "ministry of a handful," says that 20 percent of the people do the work that benefits 80 percent. As a result, the people in the 20 percent can feel used and abused and drop out in frustration or self-preservation. The 80 percent can feel disaffected or scattered. All somehow feel disconnected to discerning God's will for them in serving in their congregation.

In many congregations, people feel further disconnected due to the lack of clearly defined volunteer job descriptions and appropriate boundaries of responsibility and authority. Added to this, recruiting volunteers is sometimes seen as filling slots rather than discerning God-given gifts and offering opportunities to use them.

Adequate and relevant staffing can address the frustrations and limitations of a willing, yet challenged, volunteer pool. Staff members can be recognized and empowered to serve as leaders who enable others to discern and use their gifts, guide others to accomplish clearly defined and achievable tasks, and encourage others to work within understandable boundaries of authority and responsibility. They can help individual members of the congregation find appropriate ways to serve and use their gifts.

Overview of this book

Please note that the many legal and liability issues of employment for which the congregation is responsible should be considered with the aid of qualified professionals, since state and federal laws change over time and may vary according to the size of your church staff. Although this book may help you to identify legal questions that need to be addressed in your congregation, obtain specific advice from local counsel for these issues.

The five chapters of this book focus on mission, ministry, service, discipleship, and leadership. Each chapter ends with a section that will allow you to "Think it out—check it out" and see where your congregation is on target. Reproducible tools that relate to the chapters appear in the back of the book. The following overview highlights the main topics in each chapter.

Chapter 1: Called to Mission

The mission of the church challenges us to participate in the gospel in a changing world.
- The mission of the church
- Understanding our culture
- Staffing for mission in postmodern times

Chapter 2: Called to Ministry

Whether they are clergy or laity, called or hired, all are sent to minister alongside one another and the members of their congregations. This shared ministry requires planning.
- Using fair and equitable personnel policies
- Planning for shared ministry on your staff
- Developing job descriptions
- Remuneration and support
- Withholding and tax requirements

Chapter 3: Called to Service

Just as the staff carries out responsibilities on behalf of the congregation, the congregation has responsibilities to carry out on behalf of the staff.
- Recruitment
- Interviews
- Calling or hiring
- Employment and the workplace
- Staff support
- Lifelong learning
- Evaluation
- Corrective action and dismissal
- Changes in the staff team

Chapter 4: Called to Discipleship

Staff members are called to discipleship individually and as a team.

- Loving God
- Loving one another
- Growing in faith
- Effectively using gifts
- Called to discipleship together

Chapter 5: Called to Leadership

Staff members work with clergy and lay leaders in the congregation and serve as leaders themselves.

- Staff leadership
- The head of staff
- Staff leaders and volunteer leaders

This book is for pastors, congregation councils and presidents, committee members and chairs, and staff members. Using this book, pastors can consider needs for new staff members, ways to interact with an existing staff, and necessary safeguards for staff members. Your council can look at strategic planning for staffing, your congregation's organizational structure and where the staff fits in, and your legal and organizational responsibilities to staff members. Committee members and chairs can learn how to better work with the staff of a congregation through leadership development and a shared understanding of authority lines and clear boundaries. Staff members can use this book to challenge themselves to mission, ministry, service, discipleship, and leadership.

Individually or in a group, use the checklists at the end of each chapter to answer the following questions:

- What is going well in our congregation? Do we act in ways that are consistent with the basic values and principles discussed in this chapter?

- Based on this chapter, does our congregation have any areas for improvement or important responsibilities that are not being carried out at this time?
- How can you celebrate what is going well? What are the next steps to be taken in any areas for improvement or change?

Chapter One

Called to Mission

Go therefore and make disciples of all nations, baptizing them in the name of the Father and of the Son and of the Holy Spirit, and teaching them to obey everything that I have commanded you. And remember, I am with you always, to the end of the age.

—Matthew 28:19-20

Make disciples. Baptize them. Teach them. How do people in a newly painted church on Main Street respond to the words *teach them*? How might 12 members of a congregation council, meeting on a cold winter evening in a church basement, consider the words *make disciples*? How can a Sunday morning crowd, gathered around an altar in front of stained glass windows, participate in the words *baptize them*? And what do the words *all nations* mean?

This chapter discusses the mission of the church and the changing world in which the staff and members of a congregation are called to carry out that mission.

The mission of the church

The church is called to respond to those words from Matthew with some sort of action and measure of confidence. With faithful commitment, and occasionally even great energy and enthusiasm, people through the ages, in all sorts of settings and within various denominational understandings, have come together to cooperate in that mission.

Called to be "glocal"

Leonard Sweet says that we now live in a "glocal" world, where people see relevance both locally and globally (*Soul Tsunami*, p. 107). The mission of the church is also "glocal." It calls us to reach out to those nearby and to share the gospel of Jesus Christ with the world.

We are called to a global mission, to go to "all nations." Congregations have carried out this global mission by supporting and sending missionaries into all parts of the world to share the gospel message of Jesus Christ with people who may not have heard the good news. We challenge ourselves to participate in the lives and needs of our neighbors no matter how far away.

We also are called to reach out locally with the gospel message of Jesus Christ. Only the creating and renewing work of God can answer the great needs, both spiritual and physical, of people in our neighborhoods and communities. We form evangelism groups and study information on the ages, education, income levels, and so on of the people in our neighborhoods. Hospitality committees in congregations seek to make our church buildings, worship services, and activities visitor-friendly to the neighborhood around them and the growing world of people who have had no experience with the church. We take a moment to greet visitors at a Sunday morning service and help them to feel welcome in the congregation.

Our local mission also encompasses seeing ourselves and our congregations as a people in need of the restoration and refreshment that comes through communication with God and the people of God. We participate in the gospel when we seek to make the gospel message meaningful to those immediately around us.

For more information on learning about the people in your neighborhood, see *Our Context: Exploring Our Congregation and Community.*

For insights into extending hospitality, see *Our Structure: Carrying Out the Vision.*

Called to mission together

Our number one building block, our foundation, is the mission of the gospel of Jesus Christ. We are called to be a people together, "a royal priesthood, a holy nation, God's own people, in order that

Mission statements

The mission before the entire Christian church is the basis for a congregation's mission statement.

At the same time, a mission statement can capture the uniqueness of a faith community by defining how the church's mission will be carried out in that particular congregation.

Although the central mission will be the same, the way your congregation carries it out might not be the same as a congregation in the next town or down the street or in a neighboring borough.

For more on the mission of the church and mission statements, see *Our Mission: Discovering God's Call to Us.*

you may proclaim the mighty acts of him who called you out of darkness into his marvelous light. Once you were not a people, but now you are God's people" (1 Peter 2:9-10). Particularly in the New Testament, we see examples of God's people working side-by-side to carry out the mission of the church: Paul, Barnabus, John Mark, Timothy, Dorcas, Cornelius, Lydia, Silas, Aquila, and Priscilla.

Staff members are called to mission together with each member of the congregation, with councils or other governing bodies, with committees or other working groups of volunteers, and with other staff members and clergy. This work together is carried out through prayer, by the power of the Holy Spirit, with the firm assurance of Jesus' presence with us.

Understanding our culture

The "glocal" mission of the church is carried out in a culture that is changing. In *The Once and Future Church* (Alban, 1991, pp. 8-13), Loren Mead describes the first two stages of the church as the apostolic age and the age of Christendom. The apostolic age was an age of turmoil as the early church, born in the fire of Pentecost, strove to seek its identity and answer its call to mission in a world that was hostile to its existence and development.

With the conversion of the Emperor Constantine in the fourth century, the age of Christendom began as the Empire made Christianity its official religion. The Western world reshaped itself in relationship to the church, and the church oversaw the unification of religious and secular life. The structures, activities, and even the assignments of who did what in the church changed in response to the shifting boundaries around the church and its local parishes.

There are different viewpoints on when (or if) this Christian era ended, but scholars often describe the mid-20th century as the turning point in the United States. The relaxing of blue laws (previously established in support of religious custom) that allowed stores and theaters to be open on Sundays, along with the increased attraction of Eastern religions and New Age philosophies, have signaled a change.

However you choose to time such a shift in paradigms, the church's influence on U.S. society lost ground by the late 20th century. Mainline church denominations now struggle for membership. Being "born and raised" a Lutheran (or Methodist, or Presbyterian—you fill in the blank) does not mean you will attend a congregation in that denomination as an adult. Your neighbor might not attend any church at all or could reflect the growing trend of "church-shopper" or "church-hopper."

Modernism and postmodernism

As the church has moved away from being a central force in American culture, congregations have found themselves existing and working in a highly secularized world. Congregations that have succeeded and grown are often those that have redefined themselves. The societal movement from "modernism" to what many people call "postmodernism" has impacted the church as well as the culture.

This transition is not as simple as the transition from using a typewriter to using a computer or the Internet (with voice activation making leaps and bounds daily), although technology can make us dramatically aware of the shifts going on around us. Those Americans born after World War II grew up in a world with television, frozen food, radar, portable typewriters, credit cards, clothes dryers, air conditioners, and contact lenses that their parents never imagined while growing up. Today, their children have grown up in a world with day-care centers, computer dating, CDs, DVDs, laser eye surgery, cell phones, and cloning.

There have also been dramatic shifts in jobs and occupations during this time. In *Managing for the Future* (New York: Truman Talley Books/Dutton, 1992, pp. 331-332), Peter Drucker notes that in 1913 domestic servants made up 30 percent of the population. Now they are almost non-existent. The number of blue-collar workers in the Unites States has shrunk by one-third in the last two decades, while the number of farmers has fallen to 3 percent of the population. The information worker has become the emergent worker of our time.

There have been changes in the church as well. Church growth experts tell of a great decline in mainline denominations since the 1960s. Each denomination has experienced a decline in membership as a percentage of the population in the United States. In addition, the people in the pews (and in the pulpits) are aging.

Modernism, or the period we are exiting, has been a time of rationalism, scientific advancement, strict organization, analysis and control, hierarchies, bureaucracies, an emphasis on titles and credentials, the separation between work and play, and most significantly, separating out the sacred.

> While surveys tell us that more Americans than ever are interested in spirituality, young adults, single adults, and couples without children, ages 30 to 40, are missing from the membership of mainline churches today.

Emerging postmodernism is beginning to show some distinct characteristics. The good news is that some of these are actually "user-friendly" to the church. George Cladis provides a list of "postmodern characteristics" in *Leading the Team-Based Church* (New York: Jossey-Bass, 1999, p. 19).

- Creation is an organism rather than a machine.
- Hierarchical structures are reduced.
- Authority is based on trust.
- Effective leadership is visionary.
- Life and work are spiritually rooted.
- Structures are smaller; networks are bigger.
- Innovation is rewarded.
- Work follows gifts, and gifts are used collaboratively.
- Mainline church domination has ended.

Staffing for mission in postmodern times

"Change Is Inevitable—Growth Is Optional," reads a poster. Most of us begin to panic when we think about change. Like the character Haw in Spencer Johnson's *Who Moved My Cheese? An Amazing Way to Deal with Change in Your Work and in Your Life* (New York: Putnam, 1998) we would like to just stand still and believe that everything will go back to the way it was . . . but we all know that does not happen.

Like Haw, we eventually need to get up and move to survive. The church of the future will be a church that considers its mission in an ever-changing world. It will need to staff itself differently. It will need to reach and serve people whose lives do not resemble those of the past. If we accept that the church itself has always changed and that change is inevitable, then we will be open to staffing our congregations in ways that help them grow and look for new skill sets with which to reach the world and invite it to hear our message.

The church of the future will need to staff itself differently.

A healthy congregation is capable of reaching outside of itself, to look ahead for the next curve, and pray for God's guidance. This is an exciting time of new possibilities for the church. The local congregation is challenged to be both faithful to its gospel call and responsive to shifts in culture. In today's world, church staff members need to understand the nature of the changing cultural winds—and the force that those external pressures place upon their particular congregation and its members. They need to observe the world as it is, not be swayed by it, and minister to it through the never-changing message of the gospel.

Organizing principles for a congregation's staff need to include prayerful discernment and a steadfast determination to serve and equip the congregation for mission amid a windstorm of change. Congregations need staff members who can communicate the way through the changes ahead, hold high the vision of the congregation, and invite the congregation to unite under that vision.

How will postmodernism affect the staffing of congregations?

Models of staffing in the postmodern world will need to take into account current trends in business and academic circles regarding how people receive and retain information. These trends suggest that as visualization and relational sharing increase, people are more involved and their ability to retain information grows exponentially.

- Christian education staff members will use new technologies to achieve active visualization and moving imagery as a tool to teach Christian principles and Bible stories.
- Evangelism directors will reach out with welcoming words that recognize the church as a "family," and yet include one of the fastest growing segments of our society—single heads of households. They will develop ways to share faith that speak to people who have little or no experience with the church.

- Facilities managers will understand the relational and community aspect of congregational life and will work to make church spaces open and hospitable (for instance, by using round tables that model connections between people). They will seek to meet the demands the new world view will put on church facilities.

- Music directors will work in collaboration with pastors and the media staff to make worship a time of communal participation for those who attend services. They will facilitate encounters with both old and new liturgical expressions.

- Heads of staff will recruit staff members whose ages and ethnic backgrounds mesh with the people they hope to reach, both in the pews and in the streets. (The 2002 U.S. census reports that 40 percent of the population under the age of 18 identify themselves as one of the following groups: American Indian or Alaska Native; Asian; Black or African American; Native Hawaiian or Pacific Islander; Hispanic or Latino.) They will engage staff members in building a vision and see the development of authentic Christian relationships as important as the accomplishment of tasks.

- Program directors will redefine specialized areas to incorporate changing demographics and scan the horizons for inventive ways to speak good-news words. The range of senior ministry will mushroom to address the aging of baby boomers, while youth ministry will utilize chat rooms and visual imagery.

- Small group leaders will link with other denominations, making the gospel message more central to sharing and learning techniques than the particular denomination of the small group. They will link the longing for connectedness and shared values to genuine relationships and meaningful service in small group experiences.

Think it out—check it out

Use the
"Staff Exercises
on Mission"
tool on pages
87-88 to build
your staff team.

- Our congregation understands the mission of the gospel of Jesus Christ and its call to be "glocal."
- Members of our congregation and the staff team actively seek to understand and respond to the changing culture in which the church is called to serve.
- Our congregation recruits staff members who have appropriate skill sets for carrying out the mission in the world we are called to reach.
- Members of our congregation and the staff team work together to proclaim the unchanging message of Jesus Christ in an ever-changing world.

Chapter Two

Called to Ministry

Each church denomination has a unique understanding of clergy and laity. For Lutherans, the ordained ministry of pastors is the ministry of word and sacrament, while associates in ministry, deaconesses, and diaconal ministers are in the ministry of word and service. Pastors, associates in ministry, deaconesses, and diaconal ministers are *called* to congregations. Others are commissioned to do works of service and fellowship. They are *hired* as staff. Retired clergy members also may be hired by the congregation.

Whether they are clergy or laity, called or hired, all staff members are sent to minister alongside one another and the members of their congregations. This shared ministry requires a great deal of planning before recruiting and interviewing for a new staff member or new position ever begin. This chapter will look at calling or hiring procedures and personnel policies, staff configurations, job descriptions, and remuneration and support.

Using fair and equitable personnel policies

When a congregation does not have clearly written expectations for the calling or hiring of lay staff members, the process can vary from one person to the next. These variations in these procedures can result in conflict within a staff. (If the call process for an additional pastor varies from that used for the senior pastor position, this can be a problem as well.) To prevent this type of conflict, develop an equitable and standardized process for calling or hiring lay staff members as part of the personnel policies for your congregation.

In the Evangelical Lutheran Church in America, procedures for the employment, corrective action, and termination of rostered individuals (pastors, associates in ministry, deaconesses, and diaconal ministers) are provided in the governing documents of the denomination, synods, and congregations.

Members of ELCA congregation councils should familiarize themselves with these procedures. Legal courts will rarely interfere with the way a congregation, synod, or denomination handles employment matters related to rostered individuals unless the procedures in the governing documents are not followed.

Personnel policies need to be written in compliance with local, state, and federal laws and in accordance with the governing documents of the congregation, the synod or judicatory, and denomination. Effective personnel policies are written in equitable and balanced support of both the congregation as an employer and the staff members as employees. Policies should include, but need not be limited to, the congregation's mission, vision, and employment philosophy; procedures for determining employee salaries and benefits; evaluation and problem resolution; employee rules, regulations, and safety issues; procedures for recruiting, calling or hiring, and firing; job and role clarifications; and organizational structure.

Writing or revising personnel policies can help everyone to understand how the congregation relates to its staff, how staff members relate to each other, and how staff members relate to the leaders and congregation. Seek legal counsel for assistance in writing and reviewing your congregation's policies. Synod or judicatory staff members and human resources specialists can also provide you with more information. See the "Personnel Policies" tool on pages 89-93 for a list of topics that you may want to include in personnel policies for your congregation.

Planning for shared ministry on your staff

Before taking a trip, we might buy necessities and some new clothes, pack our suitcases full, hop on-line or stop by the bank for traveler's checks, call ahead for a comfy room, and plan the quickest route. Jesus prepared the disciples for a journey by calling them together and giving them specific instructions for the tasks ahead:

> He called the twelve and began to send them out two by two, and gave them authority over the unclean spirits. He ordered them to take nothing for their journey except a staff; no bread, no bag, no money in their belts; but to wear sandals and not to put on two tunics.
>
> —Mark 6:7-9

The disciples went out according to Jesus' instructions, cast out demons, and anointed and healed the sick (Mark 6:13). They were successful in their mission. The plans fit the task.

The way we configure staffing in congregations should match what we are called to do, rather than any preconceived notions of what church staffs should look like. Rather than calling or hiring to fill a position as it was in the past, consider the task *ahead*. Think about the specific tasks that need to be accomplished and how each position fits with the mission of the congregation. Above all, immerse these plans in prayer.

How large a staff is needed?

The size of a congregation's staff is often discussed in terms of the size of the congregation. In the 1960s, one full-time church staff position for each 300 active members was seen as an appropriate ratio for effective ministry. Church-growth facilitators now set a benchmark range at 100 to 150 active members per full-time position. This ratio can be helpful as a starting point, but it has been in flux for 40 years and should not be seen as static.

Consider the task *ahead*.

The size of a staff is more appropriately discussed in terms of mission and the vision that a congregation has developed to achieve that mission. If a congregation plans to position itself for a specific ministry that reaches into its community, that outreach probably should be included in a staff member's job description. Does the vision statement include developing or implementing a specific style of worship? That task also can be visible in the configuration of the staff.

What skills are needed?

Jobs should be oriented to fit the tasks to be fulfilled.

Consider the skill sets needed to fulfill the congregation's mission and vision. If a congregation decides to offer a contemporary worship service, the musicians hired should have training or experience in contemporary music and the ability to use the instruments, digital keyboards, sound boards, and perhaps digital projection equipment and software. These skills might be different from those found in an organist, choir director, or other position. If a congregation sets a high priority on reaching young people, the church staff will include positions that call for specific skills needed to reach and communicate with youth.

Jobs should be oriented to fit the tasks to be fulfilled, not just positions or titles. New positions, or new ways of looking at old positions, will probably require new skill sets.

Will a position equip people or provide support?

Think carefully about whether a new position will equip people for ministry or build support systems. Both types of positions are needed on staff.

When and where will the work be done?

Should a position be full-time or part-time? Think creatively about positions with time frames that respond to needs, rather than the clock or calendar. Think about where the work needs to be done as well. Some work may be done at home, out in the community, or in the homes of congregational members, as well as in the church building.

How would a new position fit with your staff?

What is the configuration of the existing staff? What are the personalities, goals, and working styles of current staff members? Is teamwork important to the staff or do members work as individuals? Consider these questions as you plan or prepare for a new position or new staff member.

Developing job descriptions

Once you have considered the previous questions about configuring your staff, job descriptions should be developed to fit the tasks that need to be accomplished. Resist the temptation to think only about what positions have been called or how they have been carried out in the past. Think about the desired outcome, the big picture, and the congregation's goals. Then write down specific tasks needed to accomplish those goals. Provide job descriptions for everyone on the church staff, including existing staff members, new positions, and full-time or part-time positions. See the "Sample Job Description" tool on pages 94-97. Well-written job descriptions and titles can become dynamic and timely tools, rather than limitations or generalities, for staff members and the congregation.

Provide job descriptions for everyone on the church staff.

A SMART job description

A SMART job description will be *specific, measurable,* show clear *authority* and accountability lines, include *realistic* goals, and work within a *time* frame.

Identify specific tasks, duties, responsibilities, and the job title for the position; any areas that overlap with other positions or ministries;

and the resources and budgetary funds available for the position. Also distinguish between essential and non-essential functions regarding the physical aspects of the job.

Define measurable standards that will be used in staff evaluations. These standards should relate the tasks, duties, and responsibilities of the position to the mission and vision of the congregation.

Clarify authority and accountability by describing the working relationships with other members of the staff and working groups within the congregation. For the development of effective and efficient ministry and good team dynamics, a regular full-time staff member should report to a staff member, not to a volunteer. If staff members report to volunteer leaders, boundaries between the pastoral leadership, staff members, and volunteers can be blurred. This can eventually erode the productivity and trust levels needed by a proficient staff team. The only exceptions to this guideline are short-term or contractual employees, who might be overseen by and report to a volunteer. For example, someone hired to catalog and organize the church library (a short-term employee) might report to the chair of the education committee, while a person hired for cleaning or landscaping (a contractual employee) might report to the chair of the facilities committee. Clear boundaries can be illustrated by charting the lines of authority and responsibility between staff members and ministries. Use the "Lines of Authority and Responsibility" tool on pages 98-100 to review an existing chart or create one for your congregation.

Include realistic goals that are achievable in the current situation. The members of a congregation may have expectations based on how someone else did a certain job or how it was done in another place. Providing realistic goals in a job description can provide motivation for the staff member and build mutual respect between the staff member and congregation.

Provide the time frame in which tasks are to be accomplished. This includes the duration of the job, number of hours on the job,

Job descriptions are works in progress because they reflect tasks to be accomplished in ministries that will change and grow. Review job descriptions regularly, perhaps as part of the annual evaluation process for each staff member.

When the nature of the job changes, these changes should be recorded in the job description. This provides for flexibility in the congregation's ministries. It also allows for the creativity and growth of staff members and for their strengths to be best used for the ministries of the congregation.

Some duties may need to be reassigned or intentionally left behind when changes are made in job descriptions.

specific daily and hourly schedules, deadline responsibilities, and annual or seasonal obligations. The person who will supervise a position should be involved in developing the job description or duties for that position, along with representatives from appropriate areas in the congregation's ministries.

Remuneration and support

Once a job description is developed in light of the overall strategic mission of the congregation, funds for the position will need to be made available by the council and congregation to cover salaries, benefits, and expenses. No staff member may be called or hired without the allocation of funds to pay that employee. Funds may also be needed to provide the appropriate space, furniture, equipment, and supplies for the position.

Developing a new position or calling or hiring a new person to a vacated position should be part of intentional and strategic planning in the congregation. With an understanding of your congregation's mission, vision, and need for staff members to lead in critical areas, you can begin long-range planning for staff expansion (if needed) and develop operating budgets and annual stewardship or financial programs to fulfill staffing needs.

One of the most sensitive yet vital areas of staff motivation is adequate compensation.

One of the most sensitive yet vital areas of staff motivation is adequate compensation, in part because most congregational budgets are detailed and public documents voted on by the congregation. This line-item detail can cause discomfort for both staff members and decision-makers, especially when there are great variations in staff compensation. Because inequity among the salaries of staff members can also work against individual motivation and teamwork, a rule of thumb suggests that compensation rates for each position vary no more than 15 to 20 percent from the position directly above it.

Congregations and staff members alike feel the pressures presented in paying some for work in the congregation. Some members may feel that staff members work for the good of the gospel and therefore should need only minimal compensation, while others believe that good workers should receive good pay for a good job accomplished and may consider setting up merit pay scales. This tension takes place within an organization that relies on donors for its resources. This means that the congregation may struggle to expand resources for increasing ministry and staff needs or deal with conflicting beliefs from members on how to delegate resources for staffing and other areas. Congregational leaders can use the mission and vision of the congregation, as well as intentional strategic planning, to unite rather than confuse, frustrate or alienate members of the congregation when decisions are made about the allocation of resources.

Salaries

In the Evangelical Lutheran Church in America, annual salary guidelines for associates in ministry, deaconesses, diaconal ministers, and clergy are provided by the local synod. These guidelines usually include low to high salary ranges and take into account years of service, educational background, and any housing provisions. If you are not in an ELCA congregation, check with your judicatory offices for guidelines.

Salary guidelines for other staff members can also be obtained. Local organist guilds can provide salary guidelines for organists and, in some cases, for paid instrumentalists. Salary guidelines for program, administrative or technical staff members were once extremely hard to find but are becoming more accessible as denominations and church service organizations have begun to collect data. See the recommended resources on pages 84-86 for more information. These salaries are generally geared to similar secular jobs within the community in which the congregation is located. In your community, other congregations (within and outside your denomination) may have similar staffing needs and much to share for comparison purposes on staff salaries and job descriptions.

When setting pay scales, take into account details of the job description such as education, skill sets, experience, and hours that will be worked (including regular preparation, setup, and rehearsal times). In newer fields with no established guild or organization to provide guidelines, special attention should be given to these criteria. As in any organization, good pay can help to keep a good staff in place, and a satisfied staff can provide longevity for the development of ministries.

The benefits package can make a staff position more attractive to candidates.

Benefits

The benefits portion of a staff member's compensation package generally includes medical, dental, accident, disability, and life insurance and a pension plan or other investment plan. Other benefits include holidays, vacation time, sick leave, reimbursements, and allowances. The benefits package can make a staff position more

Base decisions about benefits on your policy.

attractive to candidates. Consider offering flexible hours, liberal holiday and vacation schedules, and the ability to work from home as valuable time benefits that can be provided at minimal cost to the congregation.

The council or congregation should develop a policy to clarify employee eligibility for benefits, and which costs, or portions of costs, are distributed to employer or employee. Full or part-time status, longevity in the position, or job classification (program or administrative, clerical or technical, and so on) are some criteria that can be used in determining who is eligible. Ensure that policy decisions in your congregation are fair and equitable to all staff members. Take into consideration the financial resources available to the congregation. Also consider that new staff members may be called or hired or new positions may be added in the future. Make it a point to base decisions about benefits on your policy and not on the need or perceived need of one employee over another.

Allowances and reimbursements

Benefit packages for staff members can include designated amounts for housing, mileage, sabbaticals, books, continuing education classes, or uniforms or garments. Allowances provide a set amount of money to a staff member for a certain expense, such as housing, while reimbursements provide money for actual, documented costs incurred, sometimes against a verifiable amount such as mileage (as determined by the Internal Revenue Service). To offer reimbursements, a congregation must have procedures for accountability that require staff members to submit the date, place, business nature, and amount of expenses. These procedures must be applicable to expenses incurred after they are adopted.

See your local counsel and the recommended resources on pages 84-86 for additional information. If used, reimbursements and allowances should be planned as specific line items in the congregation's budget for each staff member.

Employer expenses

Other expenses incurred by a congregation as an employer are not listed as part of a staff member's compensation package, but need to be included in strategic planning and budgeting. These expenses may include worker's compensation, unemployment insurance, employer Social Security payments, or service costs such as payroll direct deposit.

Providing for temporary or substitute coverage for vacation, family and medical leave, illness, bereavement, sabbaticals, jury duty, military leave or other paid or unpaid leave time also impacts budgeting. If a temporary staffing agency is used to cover an administrative position, or a substitute organist must be found, or pastoral coverage for emergencies is required, it is wise to have these costs covered as line items in the budget or available through budgeted discretionary funds. Within the budget, clarify who has the authority and responsibility for the access and use of these funds.

Withholding and tax requirements

Congregations have the same obligation as any other employers to withhold federal income taxes from the wages of their employees, report the wages and withheld taxes, and pay the withheld taxes to the Internal Revenue Service in accordance with the applicable rules. The treasurer or person responsible for handling the congregation's pay roll should be familiar with federal, state, and local income tax requirements, forms, and procedures for handling payroll. This person should also stay up to date on tax law changes. Responsible people in the congregation who willfully fail to collect, report, or pay taxes may be personally liable.

The wage-paying congregation must have a federal Employer Identification Number. It must also obtain the appropriate forms for each employee, consult withholding tables to determine withholding amounts, and pay withheld taxes to a qualifying depository institution or federal reserve bank in a timely fashion. Finally, the congregation provides each employee with a completed Form W-2 by February 1 of the following year and submits an additional copy to the Social Security Administration before March 1.

1099 Employees

The IRS requires tax withholding only for employees. Self-employed individuals who perform services for the congregation must do their own tax withholding. At the start of the job, the congregation obtains the person's Social Security number. If the worker is paid a specified amount or more during the year, the congregation issues the person a Form 1099-MISC before February 1 of the following year, and sends a copy to the IRS by March 1 accompanied by a transmittal form (Form 1096). Contact the IRS to find out the specified amount that requires this procedure because this changes over time.

The IRS uses a 20-factor test to determine whether the workers are employed or self-employed. The central determinant is whether the congregation has the right to control the worker in the performance of the work, not just as to the end product, but also as to the details of how and in what sequence work is performed. The right to control is sufficient; the congregation need not actually exercise the right. People engaged personally to perform services on the premises subject to the direction of the pastor or other supervisors, such as the administrative assistant or secretary, generally will be considered employed. People who can have others do a job for them, such as some part-time custodians, as well as providers of services like plumbing, snowplowing, and yard care may be self-employed.

FICA

Congregations are also responsible for withholding an employee's share of Social Security taxes (Federal Insurance Contributions Act, or FICA) and submitting both the employer's and employee's share.

Unemployment taxes

Religious organizations such as congregations are exempt from federal unemployment taxes and from state unemployment taxes in many, though not all, states. Check on the requirements in your state.

Think it out—check it out

- Our congregation sees differences between clergy and laity as giftedness from God that may call us to separate functions, but also joins us in mutual ministry for the gospel.
- Our congregation has developed and follows fair and equitable personnel policies.
- Our planning for staff development or expansion incorporates the mission of the congregation, targets the task ahead, and relies on prayerful discernment.
- Each member of our congregation's staff has a SMART job description.
- Funds for calling or hiring to fill a position or add a position are considered during our budgeting and strategic planning.
- Our salary decisions take into account the skill sets required, education levels needed, work hours, and pay equity among staff members.
- Our congregation has considered, reviewed, and taken responsible steps to carry out its withholding and tax reporting obligations to its staff members as their employer.

Use the "Staff Exercises on Ministry" tool on pages 101-102 to build your staff team.

Chapter Three

Called to Service

Whether your congregation has one staff member or a clergy and lay staff team of 25 people, it is an employer. How the congregation carries out the role of employer is also an act of service in the mission and ministries of the congregation. In our society, this means serving as an employer in compliance with local, state, and federal laws, statutes, and regulations as well as constitutional, synod or judicatory, or denominational requirements. To serve in this role in the Spirit is the challenge before congregations.

Recruitment

Should you call or hire from within the congregation or outside of the congregation? Take time to think through this issue and consider the benefits and drawbacks of both options. A current member may possess all the skills, knowledge, and commitment needed, and also have relationships within the congregation that would be helpful to the position. Conversely, a current member may bring personal agendas and baggage to the job, and existing relationships may make it harder to objectively evaluate the person's skills for the job. Even if a member has a strong financial need for employment, that should not be the guiding factor in a decision to call or hire. Also consider the possibility that if a member fails in the position, he or she may choose to leave the congregation.

If you choose to call or hire from outside the congregation, network with people in other congregations and denominations to find out about individuals with the skills needed.

Interviews

With care, prayer, and diligence, you decide that a new staff member or position is needed. You determine what that person will do in relationship to the mission and vision of the congregation. The next step is to prepare for and conduct interviews.

Seek advice

State and federal laws and regulations impact the questions that can be asked of candidates and their references. Seek advice from legal counsel and human resource consultants in this area.

Include the supervisor of the position

Be certain to include the person who will supervise the new position. The supervisor should at least be involved at critical points, if not in the entire recruitment and interview process.

Consider this VIP

Consider every opportunity to interview and call or hire a new staff member as a "Very Important Possibility" to expand and lead ministry in new ways for the congregation.

Evaluate excellence and effort

There is no such thing as "good enough for church work." Develop criteria for selection based on the job description and choose the candidate who best fits those criteria.

Cast for compatibility and connectedness

When you select a new staff member, consider the personality and working styles of current staff members. Think about who the new person will work with and report to. In addition, consider whether the new staff member will be expected to make connections with certain people or groups in the congregation or community. How will this new person relate to any staff positions you plan to add in the future? Try to look ahead at the next three years.

Seek strengths and skills

Identify the strengths and skills of each candidate for a position. Because few people overcome weaknesses on the job, base your selection on the strengths of individuals. A training period may be needed so that a new staff member can develop additional skills or take on more responsibilities.

Consider character and commitment

What character traits are needed to do the specific work the position requires? The intensity of church work makes moral clarity and maturity prerequisites for a congregation's staff members.

As you speak with job candidates, look for signs of integrity, faithfulness, stability, honesty, discretion, and patience.

Make a PACT

Select people with *passion, attitude, commitment,* and the ability to work on a *team* (PACT). People who have a passion for church work, a positive attitude toward working and learning, a commitment to Jesus Christ, and the ability to work on a team will be assets to the staff and mission of a congregation.

Find out what candidates want

Interviews should also provide you with an opportunity to find out what candidates want out of a position.

Interviews should provide candidates with an understanding of the structure, mission, and vision of the congregation; the values, purposes, and principles expected and shared by the staff; and any requirement or expectation for creativity, innovation, or new skill development on the part of a new staff member. Interviews should also provide you with an opportunity to find out what candidates want out of a position, aside from compensation. This will tell you something about how they will fit into your staff.

Calling or hiring

Checking references

An integral part of calling or hiring is collecting verifiable data from others who know, have worked with or can provide information on the candidate being considered. If you receive names of possible candidates from your professional or social contacts, this information can be gathered before the interview process. Set aside time to ask your contacts the same questions you would ask of references provided by the candidate.

Regardless of how a person comes to you for the interview process, request a list of references that include professional or work-related contacts. Always follow up with each and every reference. You will want to ask some of the same questions of the reference that you ask the applicant: performance and enthusiasm on the job, specific skills, strengths and weaknesses, interpersonal and communication skills, organizational abilities, responsibilities and follow-through, decision-making and problem-solving skills, attitude and assertiveness on the job, maturity and goal-setting ability, attendance habits, and why the person is leaving a previous position. Compare the answers of the references with that of applicant. Ask the former employer (or coworker) if he or she would consider hiring (or working with) this person again in the future. Listen closely to the words the reference chooses in describing your candidate and allow for any input they might wish to add.

Always follow up with each and every reference.

Another important resource to consider, particularly when the new staff member will work with children, youth, the elderly, or in other sensitive ministry areas, is an employee screening service that can provide background checks. Be sure to choose an organization that is in compliance with local, state, and federal regulations, and one that consults law enforcement agencies for national missing persons and fugitive lists.

Anti-discrimination laws

Your legal counsel can advise you on the requirements of anti-discrimination laws in your state and municipality. If your congregation is not subject to particular laws, you still may want to consider adhering to them for the purpose of fair and ethical personnel practices.

Title VII of the Civil Rights Act of 1964, a federal statute that has been broadened by amendments, prohibits discrimination not just in hiring but in all aspects of employment (compensation, terms, conditions, privileges, and discharge) and limiting, segregating, or classifying employees or applicants in any way that would deprive them of opportunity or adversely affect their employment status. Specifically, Title VII prohibits discrimination based on race, color, religion, sex, or national origin. To be subject to the law, the employer must have 15 or more employees for each working day in each of 20 or more calendar weeks in the current or preceding calendar year, but there are exceptions to this limitation on staff size. Racial discrimination is prohibited by federal law regardless of the number of employees in an organization.

Religious organizations are exempt from the ban on religious discrimination for all their employees. However, congregations receiving federal funds may be subject to additional requirements. Child-care facilities, for example, may not discriminate on the basis of religion if they receive 80 percent or more of their revenue from grants or certificates under the Child Care and Development Block Grant of 1990.

The Equal Pay Act requires that men and women be paid equally for performing work requiring equal skill, effort, and responsibility. This act does not apply to congregations but does apply to church-related organizations engaged in commercial activities, such a running private schools.

The Pregnancy Discrimination Act extends the ban on sex discrimination to pregnancy, childbirth, or related medical conditions, treating women who are pregnant or have given birth as temporarily disabled workers. Leave must be available to fathers on the same terms.

Discrimination on the basis of intended citizenship or national origin is banned by federal law for employers of four or more workers, although an employer may select a citizen or intended citizen over an alien if both are equally qualified.

Age discrimination is prohibited against individuals over the age of 40 for employers with 20 or more employees for each working day in each of 20 or more calendar weeks in the current or preceding calendar year. Mandatory retirement for people over the age of 70 is not permitted except for individuals in bona fide executive or high policy-making positions who have certain minimum retirement benefits.

The Americans with Disabilities Act applies to employers with 15 or more employees. The act, which went into effect in July 1994, prohibits discrimination against a qualified individual with a disability if that person can perform essential job functions with reasonable accommodations that do not cause undue hardship to the employer.

The employment contract

Employment is a contractual relationship, whether or not the contract is in writing. Because contract law is almost entirely state law, it differs from state to state. In most states, unless there is some express agreement to the contrary, employment is "at will." This means that either party may terminate the employment at any time, with or without reason.

However, employers sued for wrongful termination or discipline of employees may find that employees and courts construe statements or documents other than a written employment contract as part of the agreement. This may include job advertisements, application forms, statements in interviews, job offer letters and job-related correspondence, employee handbooks, personnel manuals, and memos or notices of personnel policies or job-related matters. In addition, many states now permit exceptions to the "at will" doctrine, allowing fired employees to sue for improper discharge. Some states require that all discharges be for good cause, whether or not any specific contractual or statutory rights are involved.

Wage and hour laws

The Fair Labor Standards Act protects workers from sub-standard wages and excessive hours and regulates child labor. Most congregations will not be subject to the terms of this act but may be subject to similar state laws. However, church-related organizations, such as schools, may be covered by the federal law. This act sets a maximum 40-hour workweek unless the employee is paid time and a half for hours over 40, and it sets a minimum wage, which increases from time to time. Employees in bona fide executive, administrative, or professional capacities are exempted if certain minimum income standards are met. Congregations not subject to the act may wish to comply voluntarily as a policy of fairness to employees.

Immigration laws

The Immigration Reform and Control Act of 1986 requires all employers to verify within three days of hire that an applicant is not an illegal alien and is therefore eligible for employment. Passports, driver's licenses, Social Security cards, birth certificates, and resident alien cards can be used for verification.

The employer and employee are also required to sign form I-9 Employment Eligibility Verification, under penalty of perjury. This form, and instructions for completing it, are available through the nearest office of the Immigration and Naturalization Service. The employer must retain the form until three years from the date of hire or one year from the date of termination, whichever is later. There are no religious exemptions from this act.

Employment and the workplace

Identify, develop, and demonstrate ways to appreciate the different gifts of staff members. Help your current staff to welcome and work with new staff members in positive ways.

Staff orientation

The first day on the job is a day of new beginnings and motivation for many new staff members. Take advantage of this energy by providing the new staff person with a positive, welcoming experience that builds collegiality and connections with the rest of the staff and the congregation.

- As soon as possible, introduce the new staff member to other staff members and at worship services, council or board meetings, and committee or group meetings as appropriate.
- Provide a complete tour of the facilities operated by the congregation so the new staff member knows the location of rest rooms, lunchroom or break areas, and any available parking.
- Inform the new staff member of your congregation's safety and emergency procedures and provide any necessary security codes or keys.
- Provide the new staff member with information on the congregation's personnel policies and any expectations for procedures or behaviors. In some congregations, and many businesses as well, new staff members receive an employee handbook or copy of the personnel policies and turn in a sign-off form after reading the contents.
- Acquaint the new staff member with payroll operations, including overtime and reimbursement or allowance procedures.
- Talk to the new staff person about the date, time, and location of any start-up training.

Working environment

As an employer, the congregation is responsible for providing a working environment that contributes to the accomplishment of expected tasks. This includes maintaining clean and safe work areas, as well as adequate climate control and lighting. Suitable provisions include appropriate space, furniture, equipment, and supplies. To ensure that these aspects of the working environment can be provided into the future, an obsolescence or replacement budget for long-term capital expenditures may be needed, if one is not already in place. This is a way for lay leaders to show support of the congregation's staff members, who are the day-to-day caretakers and workers in the physical plant of the congregation.

A good working environment also includes a good people skills. Build an atmosphere of trust, respect, and open and healthy communication by developing an organizational structure with clear boundaries of authority and responsibility between staff members and the congregation. This is a gift of care and service from the congregation as employer to its staff as employees.

Maintain a positive working environment in your congregation by developing, distributing, and enforcing a policy prohibiting discrimination and harassment. If you do not have such a policy in place, legal counsel can assist you with this.

Sexual harassment is defined by federal regulations as unwelcome sexual advances, requests for favors, and other verbal, nonverbal and/or physical conduct of a sexual nature when submission to such conduct is a condition or term of an individual's employment or employment decisions or when such conduct has the purpose or effect of interfering with an individual's work performance or creating an intimidating, hostile, or offensive work environment.

Misconduct and negligence

As an employer, a congregation may be liable for damage caused by employees acting within the scope of employment or found negligent for not acting in a reasonable and prudent fashion. This liability can extend to volunteers as well.

Take steps to protect the congregation from legal liability by discussing this aspect of the employment relationship with legal counsel and managing it carefully.

- Require screenings that include checking candidate's references. Time spent here is a critical part of risk management. When appropriate, as in calling or hiring staff to work with youth of any age, outside screening agencies may be employed.
- Exercise adequate and appropriate oversight and supervision over staff members, particularly those involved in counseling and visitation. Clergy members and others who are licensed under state regulatory laws for therapists, pastoral counselors, psychologists, or other mental health professionals can be subject to secular regulation and standards of malpractice. In addition, due to the complex legal issues involved, clergy and others providing spiritual counseling should be aware of the extent and limits on the legal protection of confidentiality in counseling situations.
- Make sure that all complaints of employee misconduct are investigated promptly and thoroughly, taking into account reporting laws and confidentiality issues.

Certain categories of people must report any actual or suspected abuse to public authorities within a fixed period of time after learning of the abuse. Public authorities then carry out whatever investigation or intervention is appropriate. Failure to report may carry criminal penalties.

Because many of the regulations on misconduct and negligence exist at the state level, find out the answers to these types of questions: Who is required to report? For whom must abuse be reported?

What conditions must be reported? Who must be reported as an abuser? How and when are reports made? What is the liability for reporting or failing to report? How does the confidentiality in counseling relate to the obligation to report abuse?

You can obtain assistance in understanding state law and its application to particular circumstances from your local counsel, the state attorney general's office or department of justice, police departments and other law enforcement agencies, private or public counselors, and your synod or judicatory.

Pay special attention to situations with a higher than normal exposure to physical injury or risk such as transportation by motor vehicles, water activities, overnight trips, athletic activities, adventure trips, and gatherings of young people where alcohol, controlled drugs, and sexual activity could be present, however surreptitiously. Check with legal counsel on the use of permission slips, medical release forms, and liability release forms.

Staff support

Recognition

Recognition of work well done contributes to motivation.

Recognition of work well done contributes to motivation so that staff members feel connected to the mission, take responsibility for their ministry goals, and perceive themselves as partners worthy of support and advocacy. Different members of the staff will respond to different acknowledgements of their efforts but recognition should take place in a timely manner, with specific details, and in a way that acknowledges how the organization or others were helped. Sometimes the staff team may be acknowledged collectively.

Support systems

Mutual ministry committees

A mutual ministry committee serves as a support system by addressing issues raised by a staff member or pastor, providing feedback from the congregation, and serving as an advocate for the individual. One committee may be formed for each staff member or pastor. The congregation council president and the staff member or pastor choose those who will serve on this committee. A mutual ministry committee is responsible to the congregation council and does not generally provide evaluations or concern itself with personnel policies.

Personnel or human resource committees

In addition to mutual ministry committees, a personnel or human resource committee may be formed to develop and administer all aspects of a congregation's personnel policy, ensure compliance with governmental regulations, and serve as a practical resource for those responsible for maintaining employee files and recruiting, calling or hiring, and firing staff members. In addition, a personnel or human resource committee may provide oversight and evaluation of staff members, recommend salary advances, or serve as a facilitator and conduit for any staff issues and grievances.

All staff members should have recourse to a neutral board.

All staff members should have recourse to a neutral board. A personnel or human resource committee acting as a grievance board could provide a check and balance system for employee concerns and those of the supervisor. If there are layers of authority within the staff structure, each level is addressed in order. For example, a complaint by a preschool teacher is first addressed with the director of the preschool. If no satisfaction is found, the teacher may have recourse to the pastor or senior pastor and then to the grievance board. The layers of structure protect both the individual and the system from undue manipulation.

Support outside the congregation

The congregation should encourage staff members to get involved in formal or informal groups with other church staff members in the community, or to start such groups. Just as there are groups for pastors within a community, organist guilds and groups for school directors and other church staff members exist at the community level. Your synod or judicatory may organize meetings for program staff members in Christian education, youth, or small group ministries. Staff members also might meet with ecumenical groups to share ideas and receive support.

Lifelong learning

Evaluation of the staff is also an opportunity to evaluate the ministry of the congregation.

Lifelong learning opportunities provide staff members with new information and skills through courses and events offered by synods, denominations, seminaries, church growth organizations, colleges or universities, other educational or business organizations, and peer learning networks. Lifelong learning can help staff members grow and learn in order to communicate the gospel in the language of the people, taking into account the culture at the same time. All the ministries of a congregation can benefit from a staff that is interacting and connecting with staff members from other congregations, denominations, and educational organizations. By budgeting for continuing education and encouraging staff members to use this benefit, congregational leaders can support lifelong learning among the staff.

Evaluation

Evaluations should be done at least annually. Quarterly or more frequent informal or check-up conversations are helpful to the process. The goal is to see how ministry goals in the job description are being met. The supervisor may request or receive input from committees or ministry areas for which the staff person is responsible.

Evaluation of the staff is also an opportunity to evaluate the ministry of the congregation. Staff members represent fixed points of ministry for the congregation and should be evaluated within that larger context. If job descriptions are used as working documents, they will include helpful benchmarks and goals for staff members. As part of the evaluation process, a supervisor can help each staff member to analyze, develop, and appraise the goals for their areas of ministry.

As part of the evaluation process, supervisors should ensure that annual attendance or time records are maintained for each staff member to show time accrued and used for vacation, family leave, illness, bereavement, sabbaticals, and other paid or unpaid leave time. (Time-record forms are available from most vendors of office supplies and forms.) Time records and evaluation forms may be placed in employee files. For more information on items commonly included in these files, see the "Employee Files" tool on pages tool on 103-104. The questions listed in this tool will need to be discussed with your legal counsel because regulations vary from state to state.

Corrective action and dismissal

Poor job performance, intentionally harmful or weak communication patterns, territorial attitudes, improper behaviors or various other issues call for a more targeted approach with a staff member. Consult the governing documents of the denomination, synod, and your congregation for procedures to follow in the corrective action or dismissal of a person rostered in the ELCA. If you are not dealing with a person rostered in the ELCA, obtain legal counsel for advice on appropriate procedures and required documentation.

In general, the supervisor carries out the corrective action process, which may include a verbal warning, a written warning, a probation period, suspension, and finally termination. The staff member should be made aware of the seriousness of the procedures, while being given the opportunity and encouragement to improve. Those people involved in the decision-making process may include members of any group that serves as an advocate for the staff, as well as the supervisor of the person. The dismissal meeting with the staff member is best done by the supervisor, with at least one other person in attendance.

Dismissal is the answer when the removal of a poorly contributing staff member is a service to the mission of the congregation. In *Managing the Non-Profit Organization*, Peter Drucker points out that executives in such situations can get caught between the desires to have a competent staff and to show compassion (New York: Harper Collins, 1990, p. 154). The manipulation of constituencies built by poorly performing staff members can also become a deterrent to the mission of the whole congregation. For these reasons, dismissal of a staff member requires prayer, discernment, and fair and transparent procedures throughout the decision-making process.

If staff members and any other pastors will be required to resign when a new solo or senior pastor arrives, this must be included in the personnel policies of the congregation, letters of call, or hiring documents.

Changes in the staff team

For more on change and conflict, see Our Community: Dealing with Conflict in Our Congregation.

You may be reading this book because your staff team is currently undergoing change. Because staff members can move away, marry, divorce, look for new opportunities, make lifestyle changes, retire, and die, changes will occur in every congregation's staff. Leaders of the congregation may decide to eliminate, change, realign, or add staff positions.

Any or all of these changes can be felt throughout the entire congregation and may result in grief or conflict within the congregation. When any changes (growth or loss, lay or clergy) occur within in a congregation's staff team, it is imperative, to *communicate, communicate, communicate* those changes to the rest of the staff and to the entire congregation. It is almost impossible to ascertain ahead of time all of the areas or individuals likely to be affected by a change in the congregation's staff. This means that clear, quick, and appropriately timed communication is essential. This communication can also bring to the surface any needs or concerns that need to be addressed.

Interim ministry

In varying degrees in different synods, interim or transitional ministry for the office of pastor has become a specialized ministry area within the Evangelical Lutheran Church in America. Interim ministry can also be used during other changes on a staff team. The ELCA has two models for interim ministry.

The *change agent* model focuses on five areas to be addressed and developed within the congregation under the guidance of the interim pastor: coming to terms with history, managing leadership shifts, finding a new identity, re-establishing links with the denomination, and committing to a new future.

The *grieve, heal, and move forward* model stresses a slower and more organic process of adjustment, while allowing members to see change from one pastor to the next as positive.

After a solo or senior pastor leaves, a congregation using either model receives pastoral care in the interim period before a new pastor arrives, which can allow time to conduct the self-study and call process.

If you are in an ELCA congregation in transition between pastors or lay staff members, check with your synod for details on interim ministry.

If you are in another denomination, contact your local judicatory for information on how interim or transitional ministry is handled.

Think it out—check it out

Use the
"Staff Exercises
on Service"
tool on pages
105-106 to
build your
staff team.

- The interview process in our congregation considers candidates' strengths, skills, character, commitment, attitudes, desires, and ability to work on a team and provides candidates with specific information on our mission, organization, values, and expectations.
- Our calling or hiring decisions comply with anti-discrimination laws.
- We are committed to providing a work environment in our congregation that is free from discrimination and harassment.
- Our congregation has done intentional planning in the area of risk, safety, and liability management and obtains legal counsel when necessary.
- Our congregation provides staff members with recourse to a neutral board.
- Our congregation and staff supervisors encourage staff members to participate in support networks available to them.
- Our congregation has developed and follows fair and equitable procedures for calling or hiring, evaluation, corrective action, and dismissal.
- Clear information about staffing changes is communicated to the entire congregation.

Chapter Four

Called to Discipleship

First and foremost, all staff members of a congregation are called to be disciples of Jesus Christ. Discipleship calls for the individual spiritual growth of staff members and a healthy community life. It also serves as a powerful witness to the gospel.

As individuals and as a staff team, staff members can model discipleship in their work and relationships with each other, with the lay leaders and workers of the congregation, and in and among the entire congregation and community. God's glory and grace have not only redeemed us, but have called us to live transformed lives. How members of a congregation's staff treat one another, speak to and about one another, and resolve conflicts with each other can reflect that recreated life in Christ.

Loving God

Loving God is the basic calling of a Christian. We are called to love God, because of who God is, because God alone is worthy of such a total response, and because God first loved us (1 John 4:19). This is not about an emotional response or a regulated obligation, but a committed personal relationship with God. We are called to put God first, to answer that calling with an eager heart and to do all things for the honor and glory of God.

While it may seem that people who choose to be staff members of a congregation would automatically live out this kind of relationship, we are all challenged each day to put our relationship with God first in our lives. Staff members can seek to do this in personal prayer time; regular Scripture reading; corporate worship; time, talent, treasure, and other life decisions; and service to others.

Personal prayer time

We can put God first in our lives by committing to a regular time of prayer, anticipating that as we speak and listen to God we will grow in appreciation of the power, holiness, and glory of God.

Regular Bible reading

We can put God first in our lives by committing to regular Scripture reading, allowing God to reveal the wisdom and power of the Word.

Inextricably bound together with loving God is the call to love one another.

Corporate worship

We can put God first in our lives by committing to experiencing the unique connection developed within the body of Christ during corporate worship. By participating in the sacraments we can receive the grace of a loving, living, and fully present God.

Time, talent, treasure, and other life decisions

We can put God first in our lives by committing to prayerfully consider the use of our time, gifts, money, and possessions under the scriptural model of giving our first and best to God and by individually seeking God's will before our own.

Service to others

We can put God first in our lives by committing to serve others and share God's love with them.

Loving one another

Inextricably bound together with loving God is the call to love one another. Being called to love one another, however, requires that two (or more) imperfect humans will be involved. As Christians, being called to love one another means that we will become involved with—in fact, bump into daily and sometimes painfully—all the weaknesses and frailties that make up our human nature.

Conflicts will happen, as we see in Matthew 18:15-16: "If another member of the church sins against you, go and point out the fault when the two of you are alone. If the member listens to you, you have regained that one. But if you are not listened to, take one or two others along with you, so that every word may be confirmed by the evidence of two or three witnesses." We treat one another with respect by placing that person who has sinned against us first in the matter (no grumbling or gossiping to a third party) and working together to resolve issues if possible.

Loving one another requires a degree of commitment, dedication, and energy on our part. God transforms, renews, and heals relationships in ways that speak of the glory of God. Christian love involves commitment and action. A staff team can show love for one another by calling upon the grace and power of the Holy Spirit to do the following:

> Members of a congregation's staff are called to grow in faith as individuals and as a staff team.

- Honor each other's feelings, time, and gifts.
- Show respect by speaking well of one another.
- Hold one another accountable and allow trust to develop.
- Serve one another with an attitude of care and concern.
- Encourage and bless one another.
- Forgive one another and agree to work through problems.
- Make time for fellowship, worship, and prayer together.

Growing in faith

Members of a congregation's staff are called to grow in faith as individuals and as a staff team. Faith is personal, but it does not exist in isolation. By grace, we first learn about faith through others. By grace, we share that faith with others. The members of a church staff can grow in faith together by encouraging one another and admonishing one another to faith: "Let the word of Christ dwell in you richly; teach and admonish one another in all wisdom" (Colossians 3:16).

We need to be honest with ourselves and with each other and recognize that we will have problems in living out our faith. We can recognize and help one another to discern and overcome obstacles on our faith paths. Becoming spiritually mature means intentionally seeking to grow into the likeness of Christ, both as individual children of God and as members of the body of Christ. As we pray, read Scripture, hear God's word, come together as the body of Christ, and receive the sacraments, we will find a variety of hindrances to our growth. We live in a world where widespread ideas often oppose the values of the kingdom of God. We can struggle with doubts about our faith. We can feel trapped by our human nature and old patterns and habits of wrongdoing or sin. We can find ourselves plagued by fears, temptations, and anxieties. We can be overcome by pride, selfishness, or envy. We can indulge in guilt, gossiping, resentments, greed, or a myriad of other human weaknesses.

God is greater than all of our weaknesses.

A member of the church staff may also become an obstacle in the path of another on the staff team. Although the weaknesses or conflicts of staff members can ricochet throughout the congregation, God is greater than all of our weaknesses and gives us the power to overcome them through repentance and forgiveness.

Repentance means "to turn around" or "to be turned around." Repentance is our response to the invitation to be transformed by God's reconciling power. Ephesians 4:22-24 reminds us: "You were taught to put away your former way of life, your old self, corrupt and deluded by its lusts, and to be renewed in the spirit of your minds, and to clothe yourselves with the new self, created according to the likeness of God in true righteousness and holiness."

Repentance and the power of God's forgiveness allows us to forgive others. There is nothing more powerful than a congregation where God's forgiveness is at work in each of its members. This should begin first with members of the church staff submitting themselves to God's renewing and transforming power, day by day, obstacle by obstacle. By holding one another accountable in love to the challenges of the gospel, members of the church staff allow God to begin to grow the fruits of discipleship within them in a way that can serve as a model to the congregation.

Staff members can make a covenant or agreement to hold one another accountable to grow spiritually as individuals and as a staff team. Such covenants can be complicated formal theological documents, simple statements, or even verbal agreements. Developing a covenant can be a useful exercise for any staff team. Use the tool "Developing a Staff Covenant or Words of Agreement" on pages 107-109 to create your own covenant.

See *Growing Together: Spiritual Exercises for Church Committees* for 50 exercises that encourage the spiritual growth of individuals and church groups.

Effectively using gifts

In *The Effective Executive* (New York: HarperCollins, 1993), Peter Drucker points out that in our current work world, more workers are functioning as "executives" as they deal with information flow, rather than manual or physical output and productivity. These people need to be effective rather than just efficient. Drucker says that effectiveness can be learned so that workers have the ability to get the *right* things *done*.

This principle most certainly applies to the church staff worker. We have all been gifted by God to do the work of ministry (Romans 12:4-8). Being good stewards of those gifts means using them effectively for the ministries of the congregation. *Getting the right things done* versus simply *doing things right* is exactly what strategic planning and carrying out the vision are about in the local congregation.

There are some time-tested tools that can help a congregation's staff get the right things done. The management philosophies of Peter Drucker and Peter Senge can assist staff members in practicing sound discernment and good stewardship of the gifts with which they have been entrusted by God.

Knowing what to contribute

In congregations,
there are always
more tasks at hand
than one can do.

Staff members working within the complex organization that is the congregation need to know first and foremost what they are called to do and what they contribute to the mission of the congregation and to the advancement of the gospel. This is more than simply understanding a job description. This self-evaluation should include prayerful reflection, individual goal setting, and intentional deliberation about how the position fits into the big picture of the life and mission of the congregation. The final step is to review the results with the supervisor in a regular job analysis and honest consideration of personal performance standards. These are valuable tools for making a staff member's ministry more effective.

Knowing strengths and weakness

Staff members should take the time necessary to evaluate their individual strengths and weaknesses, how those strengths and weaknesses interact with those of other staff members, and the opportunities or hindrances those differences present in the ministries of the congregation. Lifelong learning opportunities can be used to build up individual strengths. This approach to self-development can enhance the cohesion of the ministries of the congregation by better integrating the gifts of the staff into the needs and accomplishments of the ministries of the congregation.

Prioritizing

In congregations, there are always more tasks at hand than one can do. With help from the supervisor, staff members are responsible for prioritizing their tasks, taking into account the greater ministry goals of the congregation. Prioritization can help staff members avoid the burnout that so often is part of congregational ministry. Burnout can occur not just because there is too much to do, but also because too much of what is done doesn't really need to be done or doesn't seem to matter. Forethought, integrity, and self-control are needed to develop priorities that are intentional and dedicated to the mission and vision of the congregation.

Managing time

Time management is crucial for a congregation's staff. One effective tool for managing time is a two-step process of evaluation.

Step 1: Record all the tasks you accomplish and the time each task requires. You can gather helpful information by doing this over a period of time, such as a month.

Step 2: Analyze what has been recorded. Very often, this step reveals surprising differences between what you believe has been accomplished and what is actually recorded. Analyze each task. Does it need to be done? What would happen if it did not continue? Could it be done differently? Can part of it be changed? Could someone else accomplish the task or accomplish it better? This analysis might result in a decision to change your behavior, prioritizing, communication, or the structure of your work relationships.

With prayerful discernment, staff members can reorganize and carefully delegate tasks, and learn to say "no" when appropriate. Consider building in some time to address new or innovative projects that require more time than routine tasks, but often add to the effectiveness of ministry.

For more information on establishing clear boundaries, see *Our Structure: Carrying Out the Vision*.

Decision making

The staff of a congregation will be called upon to make decisions as they work in the day-to-day ministries of the congregation. Effective decision-making requires clear boundaries of responsibility, authority, and accountability within the congregational structure.

It includes differentiating between tactical and strategic decisions, understanding the value of a clear purpose and objectives, learning how to use input and feedback from others, knowing when no decision is the best decision, communicating the decision, and implementing the decision. Communication and implementation make a good decision made by a staff member into an effective decision for the ministries of the congregation.

Called to discipleship together

The staff members of a congregation have a unique opportunity to serve as disciples together. By agreeing to come together and work in ways that exemplify Christian love, staff members follow Christ as their head and can become a unique team. The team is unique, not because of who the members are, but because of who they follow and serve together.

When staff members team up to follow Christ as their head, they see each other as equals, support one another, and share ministry. Sharing ministry takes time and determination. Staff members need to bond with each other so that a team can be formed. This happens through opportunities for staff members to interact regularly, develop mutual goals, and provide emotional and practical support for one another.

The staff team places Jesus Christ in the position of team leader.

A team has taken root when the entire group shares a vision and accomplishing something together in support of that vision is more valuable to the group than the individual projects of each staff member. The staff members of a congregation have become a team when they share vision, values, leadership, rules, principles, power, information, and time. In fact, in Christian terms, the staff team places Jesus Christ in the position of team leader.

As part of a team, staff members have certain responsibilities. Together, they extend the mission and vision of the congregation and help the members of a congregation to discern and use their

The staff is called not only to *be* a team but also to *model* themselves as a team. If team relationships and ministry work are healthy, that atmosphere will radiate throughout the entire congregation.

Conversely, if team relationships and ministry work are unhealthy, that will also affect the entire congregation. The staff team, in fact, functions as a smaller version of the congregation and its ministry. Building a strong and healthy staff team can enable members of the congregation to grow spiritually as individuals and grow communally as the body of Christ.

gifts. As individuals, each staff member is a team player working in concert with other ministries by contributing (pulling their own weight), collaborating (being flexible and cooperative), communicating (sharing and responding to information), and being assertive (expressing opinions and disagreements in an open and healthy manner). Each member of the staff also has a responsibility to know his or her area of charge and to accomplish what needs to be done in that area.

People crave honest authentic relationships. The Christian church has a unique opportunity to meet that hunger. When we learn to trust one another, despite all our sinfulness and our failures, we experience the grace of God made manifest in our community, in the body of Christ. A staff team that models trust invites a congregation into the transforming presence of God.

Think it out—check it out

Our congregation and staff team together expect and encourage individual staff members to:

- Take seriously the call to be disciples of Christ.
- Take time for regular personal prayer and Scripture reading.

Use the "Staff Exercises on Discipleship" tool on page 110 to build your staff team.

- Participate in corporate worship and consider giving the first and best to God in all aspects of life.
- Hold one another accountable and challenge one another to grow in faith.
- Make time for fellowship, worship, and prayer together.
- Commit to serving others.
- Use their gifts effectively.
- Work as a team in shared ministry.

Chapter Five

Called to Leadership

Staff members are called to be leaders and to identify and develop other leaders. This chapter explores seven areas for staff leadership, the responsibilities of a head of staff, and the relationship between staff leaders and volunteer leaders.

Staff leadership

No matter what positions they hold, staff members can lead in these areas:

1. Keeping the mission and vision before the congregation
2. Setting priorities that support the mission and vision
3. Working in agreement with other staff members and volunteers
4. Making prayer a personal and staff priority
5. Seeing giftedness as the release of the Holy Spirit's power
6. Acting as caretakers for necessary resources
7. Providing clear communication

1. Keeping the mission and vision before the congregation

The mission and vision of the congregation shape the roles and expectations. Staff members and other congregational leaders can make the mission and vision clear to the rest of the congregation, always connecting mission and vision to the gospel. Staff members as leaders help to define and implement the roles and expectations that arise from the mission and vision. Because they are in a unique position of access to the daily flow of work done by the congregation, decisions made, and changing concerns, staff members are well-positioned to hold high the banner of mission and vision and to appraise the roles and expectations as they work and lead.

Create a prominent reminder of the mission and vision of the congregation with a banner, flag, logo, motto or other visual sign.

2. Setting priorities that support the mission and vision

Decisions about the ministries of the congregation need serious consideration and direction. This involves prioritizing achievable goals in order to get the right things done in the right order and at the right time.

A congregation's staff can take the lead in setting and supporting priorities that advance the mission of the congregation, while balancing the realities and limitations of resources. Thoughtful prioritizing can help prevent volunteers from becoming fatigued or frustrated. It can also involve hard decisions to reject or postpone some ideas in order to concentrate on other goals that are the most important and achievable.

3. Working in agreement with other staff members and volunteers

Working in agreement is about team ministry. It is crucial that this exist first among the staff, then among the council, committees, other working groups, and finally among the congregation at large. Without agreement, or a sense of teamwork, the best mission and vision statements will fail. Agreement is also about setting high standards and agreeing to strive to reach them. Much of working in agreement is about sharing information and committing to productive and healthy communication.

4. Making prayer a personal and staff priority

Prayer calls us to a discipleship with Christ that propels our leadership to Christian love and service. Individual prayer and communion with God is a foundation for a lifelong pilgrimage of spiritual growth. Staff members can be encouraged to develop a personal prayer life, but we are not called to this journey alone. Prayer is also a priority for the staff team: "For where two or three are gathered in my name, I am there among them" (Matthew 18:20).

> **Prayer is also a priority for the staff team.**

5. Seeing giftedness as the work of the Holy Spirit's power

All effort, energy, and skill needed to do the work of the ministries of the congregation is linked to the work of the Holy Spirit in our lives. In 1 Corinthians 12:7 we are reminded, "To each is given the manifestation of the Spirit for the common good." The Holy Spirit that allowed the early church to respond and grow is the same Holy Spirit that empowers the church today. Staff members can lead by anticipating, recognizing, and celebrating the giftedness of each person and the release of the Holy Spirit's power in our lives and congregations.

6. Acting as caretakers for necessary resources

In addition to prayer and the power of the Spirit, staff members need other resources for their work. They may need material resources, such as appropriate facilities, furniture, equipment, and supplies, as well as financial resources. They also need training opportunities, available volunteers, and perhaps other staff members. The resources necessary for the staff's work and the ministries of the congregation generally are considered during the annual budgeting process. On behalf of the ministries and volunteers in the congregation, staff members can provide important information about needed resources for budgeting and strategic planning.

7. Providing clear communication

In our daily lives, we are bombarded with input from many sources. Staff members need to provide appropriate communication that can be heard through the din around us. "Seven times and seven ways" is the golden rule of communication: Communicate your message seven times using seven different methods.

If staff members are leading in the other six ways discussed in this chapter, decisions about what to communicate will be clear. Staff communications will be anchored to the mission of the congregation and to the shared vision of the staff and members. The need for prioritizing will be communicated as wise stewardship and concentration of ministry efforts. Communication about needed resources will be shared through the appropriate channels. In a climate of prayer, our congregational and staff communications will be seasoned with our individual need for spiritual growth.

Clear staff communication needs to take place at all levels.

Clear staff communication needs to take place at all levels: between other staff members, with the supervisor or head of staff, with committees, with councils and boards, and with the congregation. These communications should flow in all directions. Effective communication is one of the most basic elements of leadership because it enables and empowers people to participate. Staff members should see it as their duty to *communicate, communicate, communicate.*

The head of staff

In some congregations, a pastor or lay staff member serves as the head of staff. This person enables staff members to lead and serve within the congregation as a team that equips others. The head of staff may be the pastor or, in a congregation served by more than one pastor, the senior pastor. A pastor or lay staff member may serve under a senior pastor as head of staff in larger congregations.

Supervision

A head of staff can be responsible for the day-to-day supervision of staff members. This responsibility can include availability and communication, staff development and motivation, evaluation, corrective action, and dismissal.

Availability and communication

The head of staff needs to be available and accessible to staff members. Good communication is vital and should flow in both directions. The head of staff can use e-mail, memos and reports, voice mail, cell phones, and so on to stay in contact with each member of the staff and encourage staff members to stay in touch with each other, particularly as their work intersects. Staff members should be encouraged to share information about their areas of ministry with the head of staff in a timely manner. In many congregations, communication will need to be deliberately and thoughtfully planned to accommodate the varying schedules of staff members.

> The head of staff needs to be available and accessible to staff members.

Staff development and motivation

The head of staff promotes staff development by keeping competence standards high, discerning the strengths and weakness of each staff member, ensuring that necessary training and resources are available for the tasks at hand, and encouraging each member of the staff to take advantage of training opportunities.

In connection with staff development, the head of staff identifies the motivations of staff members and recognizes their achievements appropriately. Whether the acknowledgement is public or private, the head of staff is in the best position to convey the recognition of accomplishments. The head of staff will know that staff members are motivated when they participate regularly in staff activities and meetings, display creativity, build team relationships, and work in a relaxed and enjoyable atmosphere.

Evaluation

The head of staff evaluates staff members, unless there are layers of accountability. In that case, supervisors evaluate their subordinates, while reporting to the head of staff.

Corrective action and dismissal

A head of staff works closely with any problems involving a staff member's poor job performance, weak or harmful communication patterns, territorial attitudes, improper behaviors, or other issues. If the problems are not resolved and prayer, discernment, and proper procedures are used in a decision to dismiss a staff member, the head of staff should move forward in as clean and quick a fashion as possible.

The head of staff can help the team get the right things done.

Team leadership

In *Managing the Non-Profit Organization* (p. 169), Peter Drucker suggests that the only satisfactory definition of a leader is one who achieves by helping a few people to get the right things done. The head of staff can help the team get the right things done by setting an example and building the team.

Setting an example

Leading is always modeling. Leaders are called to set the example. Christian teams needs servant-leaders, leaders who know that their calling is to lead by serving. Heads of staff are called to be individuals of character and integrity who are able to build trusting relationships. They are called to be faithful to the gospel and its principles.

Leaders make themselves competent to the task at hand. This means that heads of staff need to prepare themselves, working toward excellence and high standards and expecting the same from others. Leaders are not threatened by strength in others, so heads of staff need to encourage those gifts in others that they themselves do not possess. As team leaders, heads of staff need to listen and then listen some more. They must *communicate, communicate, communicate.*

Building the team

The head of staff can encourage members of the staff team to work together in agreement and covenant, lifting the vision and mission of the congregation before the team. The head of staff can lead in creating a working culture that is collaborative, trusting, and empowering, so that it enables spiritual growth and lifelong learning. Whether or not all staff members belong to the congregation, the head of staff should serve as pastor to the staff team and oversee its spiritual health.

The head of staff sets the tone of collaboration and collegiality and facilitates connective relationships that encourage staff members to achieve success in their areas of ministry and work together. When the head of staff actively develops a healthy and capable staff team, the result is a model that can be witnessed and mirrored throughout the rest of the working groups of the congregation.

Start and end staff meetings with prayer.

The head of staff brings the staff together for regular face-to-face meetings. These meetings may include all staff members or smaller groups within the staff. The head of staff encourages staff members to see these meetings as essential and therefore mandatory for all involved. To recognize the value of the staff members' time, meetings should be well-defined, short, and to the point, with clear agendas and recognizable and expected outcomes. These meetings allow staff members to flesh out all that it means to be a team together.

As much as possible, the head of staff should structure meetings to allow each staff member to be valued as a child of God (sharing one's self) and as a servant of God in a particular ministry (sharing one's gifts) that serves the unifying mission of the congregation (sharing as the body of Christ). Start and end staff meetings with prayer, keeping in mind that difficult decisions or conversations during a meeting may also benefit from a prayer break.

Staff retreats can provide some of the same advantages of a staff meeting, but in a setting that is removed from the day-to-day activities that absorb the time of staff members.

Staff leaders and volunteer leaders

For more on volunteer leaders, see *Our Gifts: Identifying and Developing Leaders.* If you are in an ELCA congregation, also see *Called to Lead: A Handbook for Lay Leaders.*

Pastors, staff members, congregation council or board members, committee or working group chairpersons, and other group facilitators all serve in constitutional or delegated areas of leadership. This unique blend of leadership, paid and unpaid, presents one of the most interesting challenges to the congregation. Working together, staff members and volunteers become coworkers and partners in the mission and ministry of the congregation.

The role of the staff in this partnership is to make it as easy as possible for volunteers to do their work, enjoy their work, and achieve results. Staff members can do this by identifying and developing the skills of volunteers, encouraging enthusiasm, building upon individual commitment, valuing each person, providing opportunities for competent contributions by members of the congregation, and seeking out resources and training opportunities that might benefit volunteers.

The top 10 tend the tone

A management principle from Peter Drucker's *Managing the Non-Profit Organization: Practices and Principles* (New York: Harper Collins, 1990) works particularly well in congregations. If staff members focus on inspiring and guiding the leaders among the volunteers, these leaders will inspire the rest.

Staff members can search out members of the congregation for volunteer leadership and devote their time and energy into developing this group for particular ministry areas, including recruiting other volunteers. If 10 percent of the volunteer base is motivated this way, it will be able to lead and motivate other volunteers. A volunteer leader who asks a volunteer worker to fulfill a ministry need can also motivate and encourage that person through regular contact and availability.

Accountability and dependability

By virtue of employment, a paid position demands accountability and dependability. Paid staff members can serve as faithful models of responsibility, enabling volunteers who share their time and gifts with the congregation to do the same. When volunteers see themselves as empowered to work alongside staff members, they come to consider themselves as true colleagues in the work of the church. When the volunteers in a congregation are supported and nurtured by an equipping staff, their ministry becomes a source and model of grace for the congregation. They see themselves as accountable for the work they are doing in the ministries of the congregation.

Authority lines and clear boundaries

No effective ministry is ever done without clear, concise, and ongoing communications that provide clear boundaries of responsibility, authority, and accountability. This includes clear boundaries for all types of working relationships—staff to staff, staff to committees or working groups, and staff to council or board.

Authority and responsibility always go hand in hand. The goal of these boundaries is to enable people to work successfully within the congregation. These structures within congregations provide the framework, or skeleton, for the body of Christ to accomplish its ministry at the local level.

Who has leadership authority and who has leadership responsibility? These are questions that should be answered in a congregation's constitution and bylaws. The history and culture of the congregation may influence how these documents are written and how things are actually done.

In a very large staff, layers of authority and responsibility may be helpful. For instance, preschool teachers and aides could report to the director of the preschool, who then reports to the pastor or head of staff. Other programmatic areas that fit reasonably well together could be structured this way, as could administrative or facilities areas. The overarching principle is that, with the exception of the most senior position, all paid staff members should report to paid staff members, and not to the volunteer base of the congregation.

Staff members may share leadership authority and responsibility for specific ministry areas with committees and other working groups. This requires staff members to build trusting relationships and to utilize consensus-building skills.

We are called to lead, not just in our congregations, but in a way that impacts the world.

Use the tool "Lines of Authority and Responsibility" on pages 98-100 to review or gather information on structure, authority, and responsibility in your congregation. In the process of gathering information or creating an organizational chart, you may find areas that are unclear. It is here that problems can arise. Find the areas that do not "fit" on the chart and work to clarify them. After your information on structure, authority, and responsibility is compiled, make it available to the congregation so everyone can see how things are done.

We are marked with the waters of Baptism, gathered around a mission that unites us for ministry, and called to serve in the name of Jesus Christ, reaching out beyond ourselves. We are called to lead, not just in our congregations, but in a way that impacts the world.

Think it out—check it out

Staff members in our congregation see themselves as leaders in these areas:

1. Keeping the mission and vision before the congregation
2. Setting priorities that support the mission and vision
3. Working in agreement with other staff members and volunteers
4. Making prayer a personal and staff priority
5. Seeing giftedness as the release of the power of the Holy Spirit
6. Acting as caretakers for necessary resources
7. Providing clear communication

- If our congregation has a head of staff, this person has the authority and responsibility needed to supervise the staff and build the staff team.
- Working together, staff members and volunteers are coworkers and partners in the mission and ministry of our congregation.
- Information on the structure of our congregation, including boundaries of authority and responsibility, is made available to the staff and congregation.

Use the "Staff Exercises on Leadership" tool on page 111 to build your staff team.

Recommended Resources

Books

Becker, Carol E. *Becoming Colleagues: Women and Men Serving Together in Faith.* San Francisco, Calif.: Jossey-Bass, 2000.

Berry, Erwin. *The Alban Personnel Handbook for Congregations.* Bethesda, Md.: Alban Institute, 1999.

Cladis, George. *Leading the Team-Based Church: How Pastors and Church Staffs Can Grow Together into a Powerful Fellowship of Leaders.* San Francisco, Calif.: Jossey-Bass, 1999.

Drucker, Peter F. *Managing for the Future: The 1990s and Beyond.* New York: Dutton, 1992.

_____. *Managing the Non-Profit Organization: Practices and Principles.* New York: HarperCollins, 1990.

_____. *The Effective Executive.* New York: HarperCollins, 1993.

Goodlin, Richard H. *Render Unto Caesar . . . or, Are You Having Fun Being a Church Treasurer? An Information Manual about IRS Reporting Obligations for Church Treasurers with Information about Clergy Tax Issues.* Contact Richard Goodlin at: St. Stephen's Lutheran Church, 901 Courtney Road, Baltimore, MD 21227.

Hammar, Richard R. *2002 Church and Clergy Tax Guide and CD ROM Set* (updated annually). Charlotte, N.C.: Church and Tax Law, 2002.

Jackson, Peggy M., Leslie T. White, and Melanie L. Herman. *Mission Accomplished: A Practical Guide to Risk Management for Nonprofits.* Washington, D.C.: Nonprofit Risk Management Center, 1999.

Johnson, Spencer. *Who Moved My Cheese? An Amazing Way to Deal with Change in Your Work and in Your Life.* New York: Putnam, 1998.

Maxwell, John C. *The 17 Indisputable Laws of Teamwork: Embrace Them and Empower Your Team.* Nashville: Thomas Nelson, 2001. See also www.lawsofteamwork.com

McIntosh, Gary L. *Staff Your Church for Growth: Building Team Ministry in the 21st Century.* Grand Rapids, Mich., Baker, 2000.

Mead, Loren B. *The Once and Future Church, Reinventing the Congregation for a New Mission Frontier.* Washington, D.C.: Alban Institute, 1991.

National Assembly of National Voluntary Health and Social Welfare Organizations. *Screening Volunteers to Prevent Child Sexual Abuse: A Three-Step Action Guide.* Washington, D.C.: National Assembly of National Voluntary Health and Social Welfare Organizations, 1997.

Nonprofit Risk Management Center and Nonprofits' Insurance Alliance of California. Managing Special Event Risks: Ten Steps to Safety. Washington, D.C. and Santa Cruz, Calif.: Nonprofit Risk Management Center and Nonprofits' Insurance Alliance of California, 1997.

Peterson, Eugene H. *The Message, The New Testament in Contemporary English.* Colorado Springs, Colo.: NavPress, 1993.

Seidman, Anna, and John Patterson. *Kidding Around? Be Serious! A Commitment to Safe Service Opportunities for Young People.* Washington, D.C.: Nonprofit Risk Management Center, 1999.

Senge, Peter. *The Fifth Discipline: The Art and Practice of the Learning Organization.* New York: Doubleday, 1990.

Smith, Hannah Whitall. *The Christian's Secret of a Happy Life.* Old Tappan, N.J.: Spire Books, Revell, 1976.

Sweet, Leonard. *AquaChurch.* Loveland, Colo.: Group Publishing, 1999.

_____. *Soul Tsunami: Sink or Swim in the New Millennium Culture.* Grand Rapids, Mich.: Zondervan, 1999.

Warren, Rick. *The Purpose Driven Church.* Grand Rapids, Mich.: Zondervan, 1995.

Westing, Harold J. *Church Staff Handbook: How to Build an Effective Ministry Team.* Grand Rapids, Mich.: Kregel, 1997.

Worth, B. J. *Income Tax Guide for Ministers and Religious Workers.* Winona Lake, Ind.: Evangel Publishing, 2001.

Web sites

Alban Institute (resources and reports): www.alban.org

Asbury Online Institute (courses, articles, and book reviews): www.aoi.edu

Congregational Resource Guide (a joint project of the Alban Institute and the Indianapolis Center for Congregations): www.congregationalresources.org

ELCA Department of the Secretary (guidelines on records management, including personnel files): www.elca.org/os

INJOY Group (on-line tools, mentoring clubs, and *Leadership Wired* newsletter): www.INJOY.com

Institute of Christian Leadership (legal, tax, and risk management resources): www.iclonline.com

Leadership Network (events, resources, and free e-publications): www.leadnet.org

Practical Ministry Innovations (archives and free biweekly news): www.parrishgroup.com/pmi

U.S. Department of Labor (current laws, regulations, and forms): www.dol.gov

Chapter 1 Tool

Staff Exercises on Mission

Use the staff exercises for each chapter with the entire staff or with smaller groupings of staff members. For brief time slots, such as the beginning of a meeting, one exercise could be covered. In longer time slots or retreats, use two or more exercises with time for small group discussions or journaling sessions. Include prayer with each exercise.

> Train yourself in godliness, for, while physical training is of some value, godliness is valuable in every way, holding promise for both the present life and the life to come.
>
> —1 Timothy 4:7-8

1. Read Matthew 28:19-20.
- List five ministries that the staff does in the name of your congregation.
- Keeping those ministries in mind, discuss this question: Whose mission are you doing?
- Are there differences between the mission of your congregation and the words of Jesus in Matthew 28:19-20? If so, what are the differences and what do those differences mean?

2. Write down the address and zip code of your congregation.
- What does it mean that your congregation meets or has a building in this zip code?

- Think about the neighborhood immediately around the congregation that the staff serves. List at least one way that the work of each staff member impacts the neighborhood. Is there an impact?
- Should there be an impact?

3. For an upcoming staff meeting, ask each person to bring a picture or item that represents their connection to 21st century culture. Invite staff members to explain the items they bring.
- Do these items make a difference in the work of the congregation. Should they?
- Read Romans 12:2: Does this verse have any relevance to your items or your discussion?

4. Read *Who Moved My Cheese? An Amazing Way to Deal with Change in Your Work and in Your Life*, by Spencer Johnson (New York: Putnam, 1998).
- What does change mean for the specific ministries done by the staff team?
- What would "moved cheese" would look like for your denomination?
- What would "moved cheese" look like for the larger Christian church?

Chapter 2 Tool

Personnel Policies

Personnel policies must be written in compliance with local, state, and federal laws and in accordance with the governing documents of the congregation, the synod or judicatory, and denomination. Effective personnel policies are also written in equitable and balanced support of both the congregation as an employer and the staff members as employees.

Take the time necessary to consider all the areas you need to cover in your congregation's personnel policies. A risk management and liabilities study can identify and review areas to include in your policies. Consult with legal, synod or judicatory, and human resources professionals as well.

Personnel policies should be reviewed and amended regularly, especially as new staff members are added or new laws and regulations come into existence. The policies document could be given to new members of the staff, congregation council or board to acquaint them with the congregation.

Many employers use a process for obtaining a signed acknowledgment to ensure that each employee has received and read the current edition of the personnel policies or employee handbook. This is an example of a statement for a sign-off form:

As a staff member of _____ Church,
I have read and understand all the information and
policies covered in this handbook and my responsibility to uphold them.

Your local counsel will advise you on the specific laws for your state. In many states, the appropriate procedure is to have each staff member read and sign off on this type of statement when hired. Whenever policies are updated, all staff members are asked to read and sign the updated version. In some cases, all staff members reread the personnel policies and sign off annually.

Many employee handbooks have inadvertently been construed to be binding employment contracts. Your local counsel will assist you in drafting appropriate policies and handbook language that accurately reflects the desired nature of your congregation's relationship with its employees. Because standards for employee handbooks vary widely from state to state, your local counsel can provide valuable insights into what to include in an employee handbook. The following subjects are commonly addressed in employee handbooks and personnel policies.

The congregation

Congregational history

Denominational background

Denominational requirements for the local congregation

Denominational responsibilities and connections

The congregation's mission and vision statements

The congregation's governance

The congregation's structure, including lines of authority and responsibility

Overview of values and philosophies for congregation as employer

The staff and congregation

Equal opportunity employment, including compliance
  with all anti-discrimination laws and regulations

Recruitment and hiring

Orientation and/or training

Confidentiality

Performance appraisal

Discipline and grievance

Dismissal or termination

Pastoral counseling

Personnel records

Overtime

Sexual harassment and other unlawful harassment

Child abuse and other forms of abuse

Youth safety and travel

Staff benefits

Pay schedules and staff classification

Available benefits

Eligibility for benefits

Insurance and pension plans

Reimbursement plans

Allowance plans

Vacation time

Holiday time

Short-term and long-term sick leave

Family and Medical Leave Act

Military leave

Bereavement leave

Sabbaticals or extended leaves of absence

Jury duty

Worker's compensation (if applicable)

Employment practices

Pay days and time sheets

Tax deductions and tax reports

Other payroll deductions and direct deposit

Evaluation and compensation

Work schedules, assignments, and record keeping

Meal and rest breaks

Absenteeism and lateness

Weather-related or emergency closings

Staff responsibilities

Housekeeping and maintenance issues

Building security (keys and security codes)

Parking

Personal property

Use of facilities

Reimbursements and allowance reports

Personal and long distance phone calls

E-mail and Internet use

Computer and software use

Job descriptions

Overview of each position, including primary and secondary
areas of responsibility and authority

A chart or graphic that shows responsibility and accountability
between positions

Work rules and practices

Ethics and expected behavior

Reporting unethical behavior

Accidents, injuries, and emergency procedures

Confidentiality

Dress code

Smoking, alcohol, and drugs

Family and visitors

Safety and fire regulations

Chapter 2 Tool

Sample Job Description

When developing a job description, determine which functions of the job are essential and which parts are non-essential (including any physical aspects of the job, such as lifting).

Before adopting a job description, have the draft reviewed by legal counsel or your human resources consultant to ensure that it is consistent with your state's employment laws and regulations.

Director of Christian Education

Effective August 2003
Part-Time Position: 20 hours per week
Flexible hours to include Sundays

The mission

In support of the mission and vision statements of the congregation, the Director of Christian Education will:

• Develop, implement, and oversee a creative program of education designed to assist individuals of all ages—both within the membership of the congregation and those touched by the outreach ministries of the congregation—to discover and deepen their relationship with Jesus Christ.

- Expand the learning functions of the congregation with a philosophical approach that is and remains open to utilizing and planning for new instructional techniques, cutting edge curriculum resources, and up-to-date technical and multi-media equipment.
- Serve as the staff member of the Christian Education Committee and its subgroups and, in working with the Sunday School Assistant, develop an in-depth and well-conceived program of teacher recruitment, training, and appreciation.
- Develop and plan intentional inter-generational and inter-congregational learning activities.

Job specifications

Essential
- Minimum associate's or bachelor's degree in Christian education or related area.
- A committed personal relationship with Jesus Christ and familiarity with the basic teachings of the Lutheran church.
- Classroom experience.
- Supervisory experience.
- Computer technology and Internet experience, including the use of graphic arts and motion-presentation hardware and software.
- A demonstrated ability to work as a team member within a staff.

Key responsibilities
Responsibilities for this position include the following, with the understanding that all tasks and duties will be accomplished in support of appropriate deadline responsibilities.
- Oversee, with volunteer assistants, the regular operation of Sunday school, confirmation, adult education, and vacation Bible school, including classroom staffing, space assignment,

curriculum development and selection, teacher recruitment and training, and trouble shooting. This includes regular attendance at Sunday school, confirmation, adult education, and vacation Bible school sessions.

- Work with the Christian Education Committee to develop special events, summer education programs, and regular publicity for Christian Education programs, and maintain Christian Education bulletin boards.
- Work with the Associate Pastor for Senior Ministries to develop intergenerational educational opportunities and activities that encourage senior adults to share their knowledge, experience, and expertise.

Skill development expectations
- Stay familiar with all of the ministries of this congregation.
- Maintain awareness of congregational, community, and denominational resources, and use these resources in developing Christian Education program for participants of all ages.
- Take advantage of leadership training sessions offered through the congregation and synod.
- Be available to pursue continuing education experiences in the areas of education and technology as approved by the Senior Pastor and as provided in continuing education.

Accountability and reporting

The Director will:

- Report directly to the Senior Pastor. The Director will participate in an annual review by the Senior Pastor to assess the Director's effectiveness in fulfilling the responsibilities of the position.
- Attend all appropriate meetings, retreats, and other team-building events for the program staff as assigned by the Senior Pastor.
- Conduct him or herself in a manner supportive to the whole staff.
- Participate in any ministry reporting schedules as requested by the Senior Pastor and will prepare an annual report to be included in the written annual report to the congregation distributed in conjunction with the annual congregational meeting.
- Meet regularly with the Christian Education Committee and also with its subcommittees as the staff person assigned to the area of Christian Education. The Director will be available to assist the chair of the Christian Education Committee in developing monthly agendas, writing reports of committee meetings for the congregational council, and preparing an annual budget request.

Chapter 2 Tool

Lines of Authority and Responsibility

The sample chart on page 100 shows a larger congregation with multiple staff positions and a committee-based structure. The pastor(s), staff members, and representatives on the council or governing board in your congregation can use this tool to review or create a similar chart.

Reviewing an existing chart

If your congregation has a chart or other information about the congregation's structure and lines of authority and responsibility, take time to review it. Are any updates needed? Can authority or responsibility be clarified in some way? Is the information on structure, authority, and responsibility available to the congregation?

Creating a chart for your congregation

If your congregation does not have a chart showing the congregation's structure and lines of authority and responsibility, consider creating one. (You may be able to use computer software to simplify this process.) The following steps will help you gather information.

Begin by listing the current clergy and staff positions in your congregation. For each position, identify the areas of responsibility, the authority the position carries, and to whom the position is accountable.

Next, list the congregation council, committees, boards, and other working groups in your congregation. Then identify the clergy or staff positions that relate to each of these groups.

Look for items that may be unclear. How could these items be clarified?

Compile the information you have gathered and make it available to the congregation.

In the example on page 100, staff team positions are shown on the right side of the chart, with abbreviations for several positions listed in parentheses. These abbreviations are used on the left side of the chart to indicate the clergy or staff positions that relate to each working group.

Sample lines of authority and responsibility

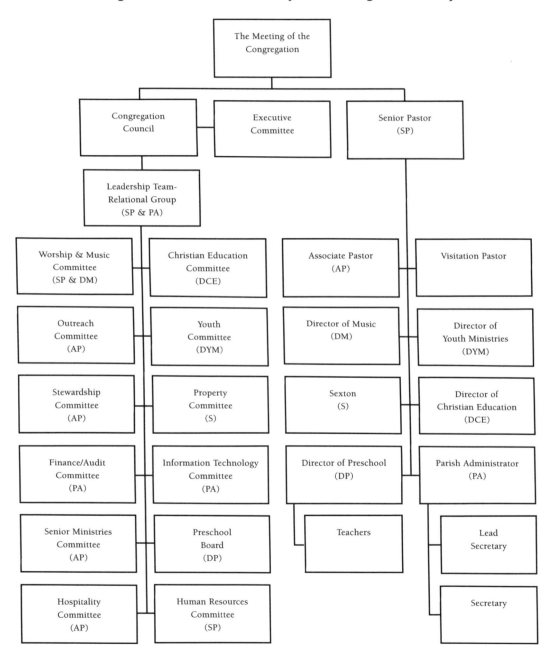

Our Staff: Building Our Human Resources, copyright © Augsburg Fortress. May be reproduced for local use. This tool can be downloaded at www.augsburgfortress.org/CLS.

Chapter 2 Tool

Staff Exercises on Ministry

1. Read Romans 12:4-8.

   Create a diagram showing how other ministries connect to that ministry. If there is time, do this with each staff member.

   - How do parts of the human body communicate with each other? How do staff members communicate with each other? Is there a connection?
   - What does it mean that we are gifted?
   - What part does learning play in a particular gift? What part does communication play in a particular gift?

2. Talk about your denomination's understanding of the differences between laity and clergy.

   - Discuss what the differences mean for each member of your staff team.
   - Are there any ministries in your congregation where it is important to maintain these distinctions? Are there any ministries in your congregation in which these distinctions are not important?

3. Talk (or dream) about the next possible new staff member or new staff position.

   - Will the existing ministries of the congregation change when this person or position is added? If so, in what ways?
   - Ask each member of the staff team to list three ways that his or her job may change with a new staff member.

4. "Comfort the afflicted and afflict the comfortable." That statement has been used in seminary training as a challenge for preachers and the words they use on behalf of the gospel message.

- What does this statement mean for other ministries in the congregation?
- What does it mean for the comfort zone of each staff member?

Chapter 3 Tool

Employee Files

Each state has different rules regarding employee files. Discuss the following topics with legal counsel. Answers will vary from state to state:

- Who should maintain an employee file for each staff member?
- What information in the employee files is private and confidential?
- What information should be included in these files during employment?
- What information must be made available to employees?
- What are the procedures for staff members to examine or copy contents of their files?
- What are the procedures for staff members to change or correct information in their files?
- What happens with employee files in the case of wrongful discipline or termination?
- What information should be retained in employee files after termination?

Items commonly found in employee files include:

- Full legal name
- Address, telephone number(s), e-mail address
- Citizenship status
- Social Security number
- Sex
- Date of birth
- Name of spouse and dependents (if any)
- Emergency medical information

- Emergency contact persons
- Date of hire or call
- Position title
- Starting pay rate and benefits available, allowances, reimbursement funds, any special provisions for vacation and sabbaticals that are not included in the standard personnel policy
- Enrollment in any special services such as payroll direct deposit
- Employment application
- Employment contracts or letters of acceptance for lay staff
- Résumé, including education and special training or skill information
- Employee's Withholding Allowance Certificate Form W-4
- Employment Eligibility Verification Form I-9, and documentation of eligibility
- Group insurance or pension information
- Current job description with position title and hours
- Record of attendance history with data for accrued and used leave time
- Signed forms for receipt or annual review of personnel policy, annual policy compliance forms, confidentiality forms, key receipts, security information receipt, and so on
- All performance appraisals
- Records of military obligation
- Formal disciplinary action documents
- Complaints or grievances from staff member
- Termination documentation

Chapter 3 Tool

Staff Exercises on Service

1. Think of three scenarios (existing or imagined) where members of the congregation's staff are, or could be, called to serve people who do not have similar backgrounds to themselves in terms of ethnic groups, religions, income levels, and so on.
- What would ministries in these scenarios look like in your particular congregation?
- What would this mean for your staff?

2. Read Mark 10:42-45.
- What is the connection between the word *great* and the word *servant*?
- What does this passage mean for your work as a staff team?

3. Discuss whether your work in the congregation as a staff more closely resembles soloists or members of an orchestra.
- If you can gather enough instruments (such harmonicas, kazoos, and so on), distribute one to each staff member. Ask all staff members to play when you count to three. What happens?
- What do you need to do in order to make harmonious sounds together? Think about preparation, priorities, order, knowledge, leadership, and listening.
- What is the next task before the staff? How can you work together in harmony on this task?

4. Read 1 Peter 4:12-14.

- Do these words resonate in your staff or in the life of your congregation?

- Have you ever felt persecuted because you are a Christian? Are you aware of the persecution of Christians in any other parts of the world?

5. Read Hebrews 12:1-2.

- What do these words say about the way you serve in the ministries of your congregation?

Chapter 4 Tool

Developing a Staff Covenant or Words of Agreement

The Bible is full of covenant language because God has made and fulfilled covenants on behalf of our redemption. Ultimately, covenants are issues of grace between God and humankind.

A staff covenant can reflect the language of God-to-humankind covenants, but it describes a person-to-person connection, helping staff members to define their working relationships and holding them accountable to one another to grow spiritually as individuals and as a staff team.

A staff covenant should not be designed as a document that excludes others in the congregation. Instead, it should provide staff members with a helpful reminder and challenge to grow as disciples: "Let the word of Christ dwell in you richly; teach and admonish one another in all wisdom" (Colossians 3:16).

Developing a staff covenant requires two things: time and commitment. Your staff covenant can be a formal theological document, a simple written statement, or a mutual verbal agreement. Use the following steps to begin this process.

1. Begin first with prayer. Ask each member of the staff to pray individually about this exercise. Then pray together, asking for God's guidance and wisdom in the covenant you will fashion as a group.

2. Look at your congregation's mission statement or vision. If this type of document does not exist, take time to think through the priorities of the congregation and list them in a short, concise fashion. Incorporate the congregation's mission and vision into your staff covenant.

3. Identify Bible passages that reflect what you need from each other to minister together and what God is encouraging you to be together. Use a concordance or some of the scriptures in this book as a starting point.

4. Next, write a statement of intent and agreement to serve together with other members of the staff and congregation in ways that allow each staff member to grow as a disciple of Jesus Christ.

   Consider including the following items in your own words.
   - Statements about your joint commitment to prayer, Scripture reading, worship, the sharing of time and gifts, and service to others.
   - Honest affirmations of availability, accountability, and responsibility to one another as staff members.
   - Words that convey and encourage trust, respect, sincere care, and concern in calling upon the staff to grow as a team in its walk together.
   - Encouragement to acknowledge one another's feelings, practice forgiveness, and follow Christian models of service.

5. When you are finished creating a covenant that all staff members agree on, share it with lay leaders and the entire congregation, perhaps in a newsletter article. Ask the leaders and congregation to hold staff members accountable to this covenant. Ask them to pray that the staff will be able to live out the agreement. Encourage each staff member to pray for the grace needed to live out the covenant.

6. At some regular interval, perhaps during an annual staff retreat, review and amend the staff covenant as needed.

7. Provide copies of your covenant to any candidates being interviewed for positions on your congregation's staff.

8. Provide copies of your staff covenant to any new members of the staff team.

Chapter 4 Tool

Staff Exercises on Discipleship

1. Read John 17:20-26.
- What does it mean to be "one"?
- What does this passage say to a staff attempting to be a team?

2. Read the Lord's Prayer in Matthew 6:9-13 or Luke 11:2-4.
- How does the Lord's Prayer order our lives?
- Read the Lord's Prayer one sentence at a time. Then write down the words that speak to you most strongly in each sentence.
- Discuss the repeated use of the word "our" in relationship to the staff praying the prayer together.

3. "We need to talk to God," reads the sign in front of a church. We do. When we have had our say, we also need to listen to the still small voice. Read 1 Kings 19:11-18.
- How and where can we hear God's voice?
- What difference does it make to talk and listen to God as a staff?

4. Discuss discipleship.
- What does discipleship mean? What does it have to do with actions, authority, and anchors for our lives?
- What does discipleship mean for the congregation and for the staff as a team?

Chapter 5 Tool

Staff Exercises on Leadership

1. Read Matthew 18:19-20.
- Do these verses say anything about teamwork?
- What do these verses mean for meeting and praying as a staff?

2. Read Matthew 18:21-22.
- Is forgiveness practiced in your congregation?
- What part does forgiveness play in your staff relationships?
- Is forgiveness a leadership trait?

3. Discuss leadership as something *that we do* and something *that we follow* as a staff.
- Who do we lead as staff members? Who do we follow? What are the differences?
- What parts do communication, learning, and relationship-building play in leadership?

4. Read Ephesians 4:11-16.
- What does this passage tell us about leadership?

5. "Born OK the First Time," a bumper sticker reads. Sin is the issue here, of course. If I'm OK, I don't need a savior or the waters of baptism.
- What language can we use to reach people who may have no concept of sin?
- What does this mean for the staff as leaders?